FRAMEWORKS OF GEOGRAPHY

DECODABLE GRAPHIC NOVEL

INTRODUCTION TO EARTH'S PROCESSES AND CHANGES

Written by Izzi Howell

Illustrated by Steve Evans

CHERRY LAKE PRESS

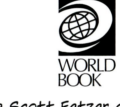

WORLD BOOK

a Scott Fetzer company
Chicago

Published in the United States of America by Cherry Lake Publishing Group
Ann Arbor, Michigan
www.cherrylakepublishing.com

Produced in partnership with World Book , Inc.
World Book, Inc.
180 North LaSalle Street
Suite 900
Chicago, Illinois 60601
USA

Illustrator: Steve Evans
Decodable Text Adaptation: Cherry Lake Press

Additional spot art by Shutterstock

Text Copyright © 2025 by Cherry Lake Publishing Group
Illustrations Copyright © 2023 by World Book, Inc.
All rights reserved. No part of this book may be reproduced or utilized
in any form or by any means without written permission from the publisher.

Cherry Lake Press is an imprint of Cherry Lake Publishing Group.

Library of Congress Cataloging-in-Publication Data has been filed and is
available at catalog.loc.gov.

Cherry Lake Publishing Group would like to acknowledge the work of the
Partnership for 21st Century Learning, a Network of Battelle for Kids.
Please visit Battelle for Kids online for more information.

Printed in the United States of America

TABLE OF CONTENTS

Changing Earth 4
Physical Weathering 6
Chemical Weathering 8
Biological Weathering 10
Erosion and Deposition 12
Water Erosion from Rainfall and Flooding ... 14
Water Erosion from Rivers 16
Water Erosion from the Sea 18
Wind Erosion 20
Ice Erosion 22
Gravity Erosion 24
Internal Processes 26
Volcanoes 28
Earthquakes 30
Human Activities That Change Earth 32
Climate Change 34
The Future 36
Can You Believe It?! 38
Words to Know 40

There is a glossary on page 40. Terms defined in the glossary are in type **that looks like this** on their first appearance. Pronunciations can be found alongside their first appearance.

CHANGING EARTH

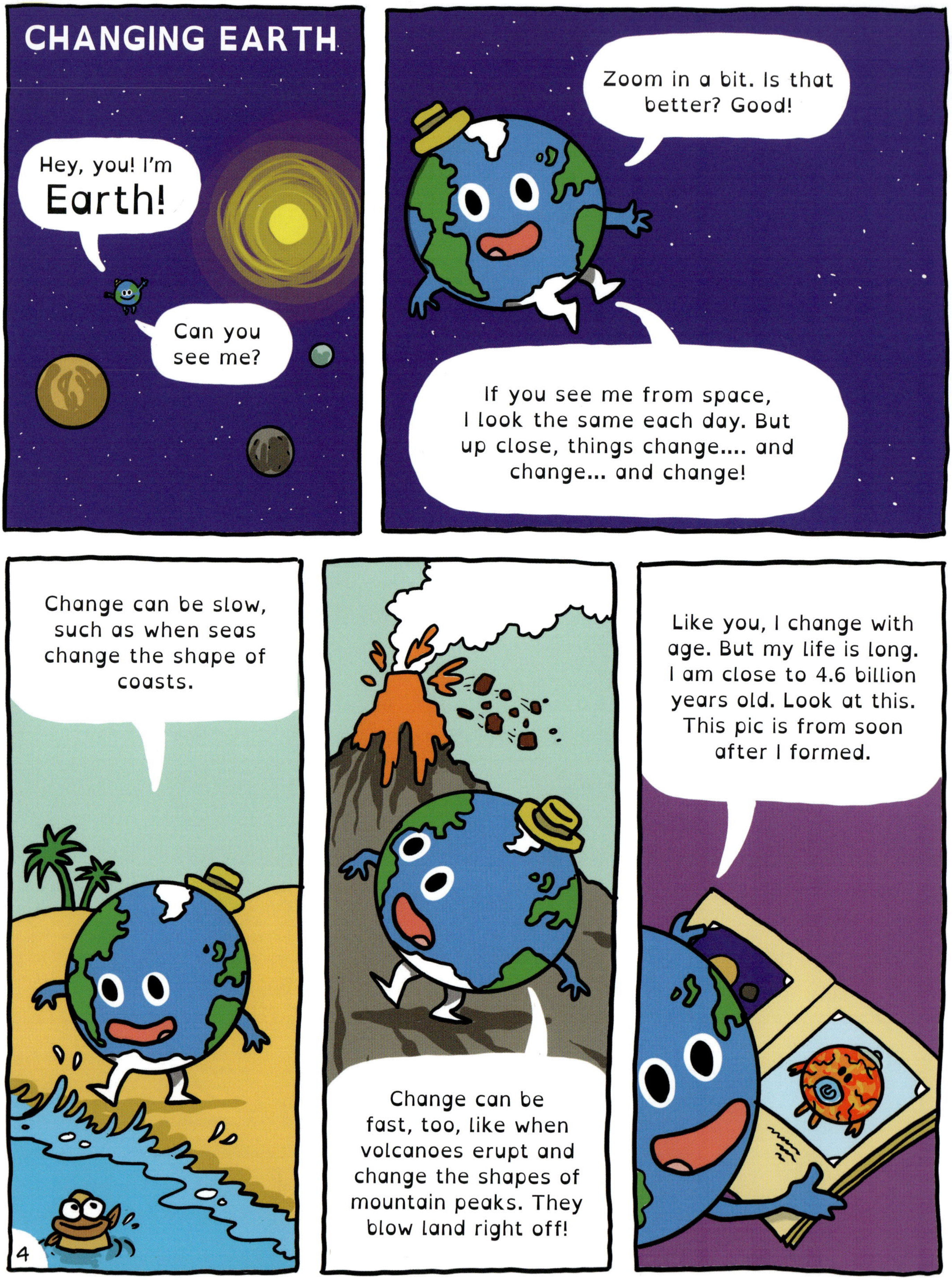

Hey, you! I'm Earth!
Can you see me?
Zoom in a bit. Is that better? Good!
If you see me from space, I look the same each day. But up close, things change.... and change... and change!
Change can be slow, such as when seas change the shape of coasts.
Change can be fast, too, like when volcanoes erupt and change the shapes of mountain peaks. They blow land right off!
Like you, I change with age. But my life is long. I am close to 4.6 billion years old. Look at this. This pic is from soon after I formed.

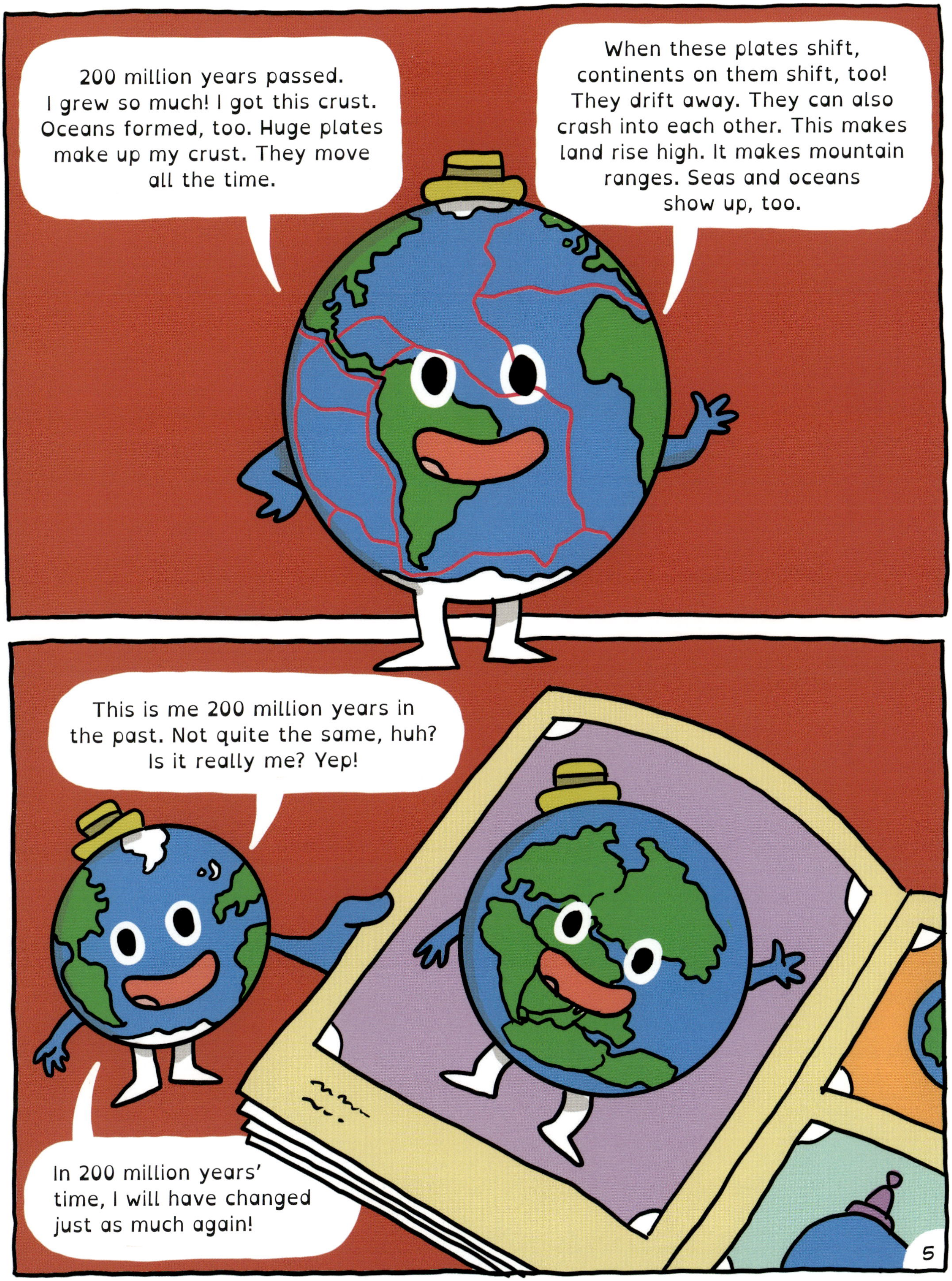
200 million years passed. I grew so much! I got this crust. Oceans formed, too. Huge plates make up my crust. They move all the time.
When these plates shift, continents on them shift, too! They drift away. They can also crash into each other. This makes land rise high. It makes mountain ranges. Seas and oceans show up, too.
This is me 200 million years in the past. Not quite the same, huh? Is it really me? Yep!
In 200 million years' time, I will have changed just as much again!

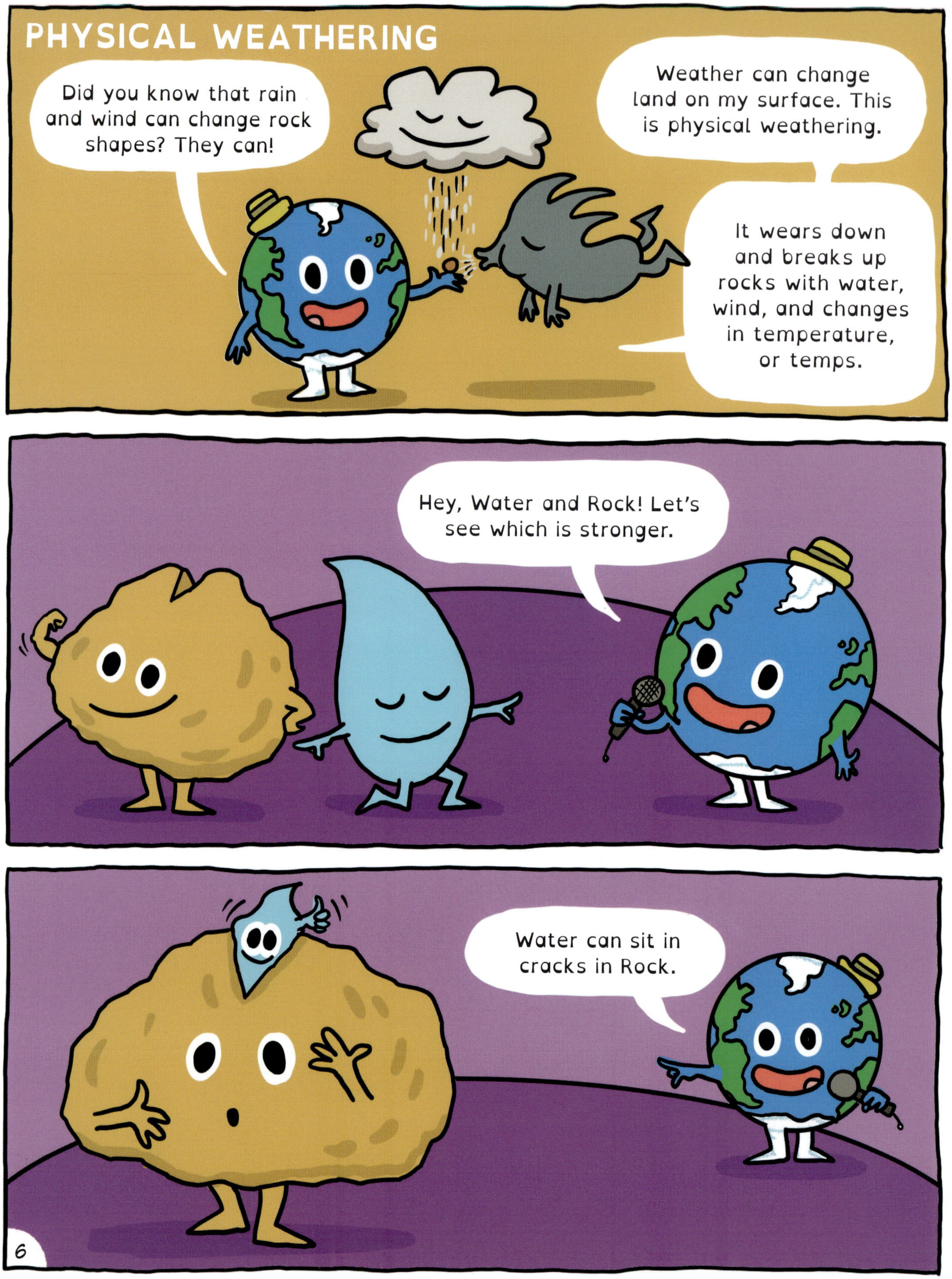
PHYSICAL WEATHERING
Did you know that rain and wind can change rock shapes? They can!
Weather can change land on my surface. This is physical weathering.
It wears down and breaks up rocks with water, wind, and changes in temperature, or temps.
Hey, Water and Rock! Let's see which is stronger.
Water can sit in cracks in Rock.

I can freeze. Then I am ice. This makes my volume grow close to 9%. As ice, I get too big for this crack. I push it apart. Then this crack grows.
Ice can then thaw. More water can fit in the bigger crack. Then it can freeze again. This can repeat. That crack will get much bigger. This is freeze-thaw weathering.
Did you think Water would win? It did! In this way, Rock is not as strong as Water.
Temps change. This can cause physical weathering, too. I get big, or expand, in heat...
...and get small in the cold.
This makes cracks show up in me. Then freeze-thaw weathering can make these cracks grow.
Wind can cause physical weathering. Wind blows sand grains and small bits of rock and dirt. It can wear rocks down. It can change rock shapes.
Waves beat on coasts. Each beach and cliff you see was made through millions of years of this type of weathering.

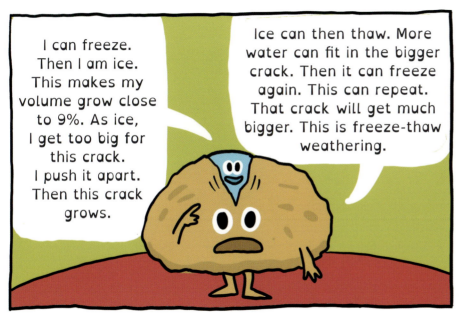

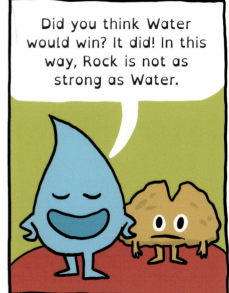

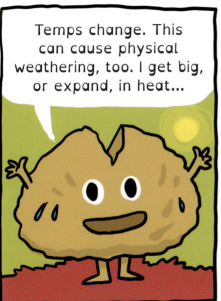

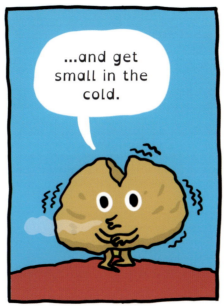

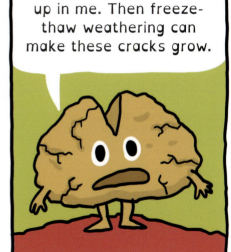

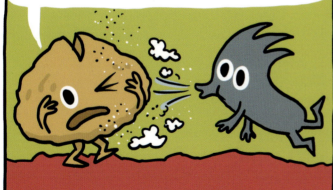

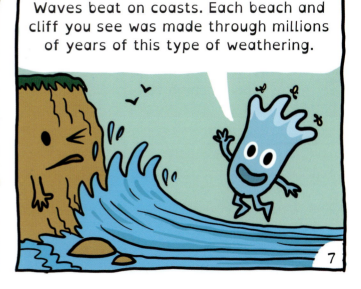

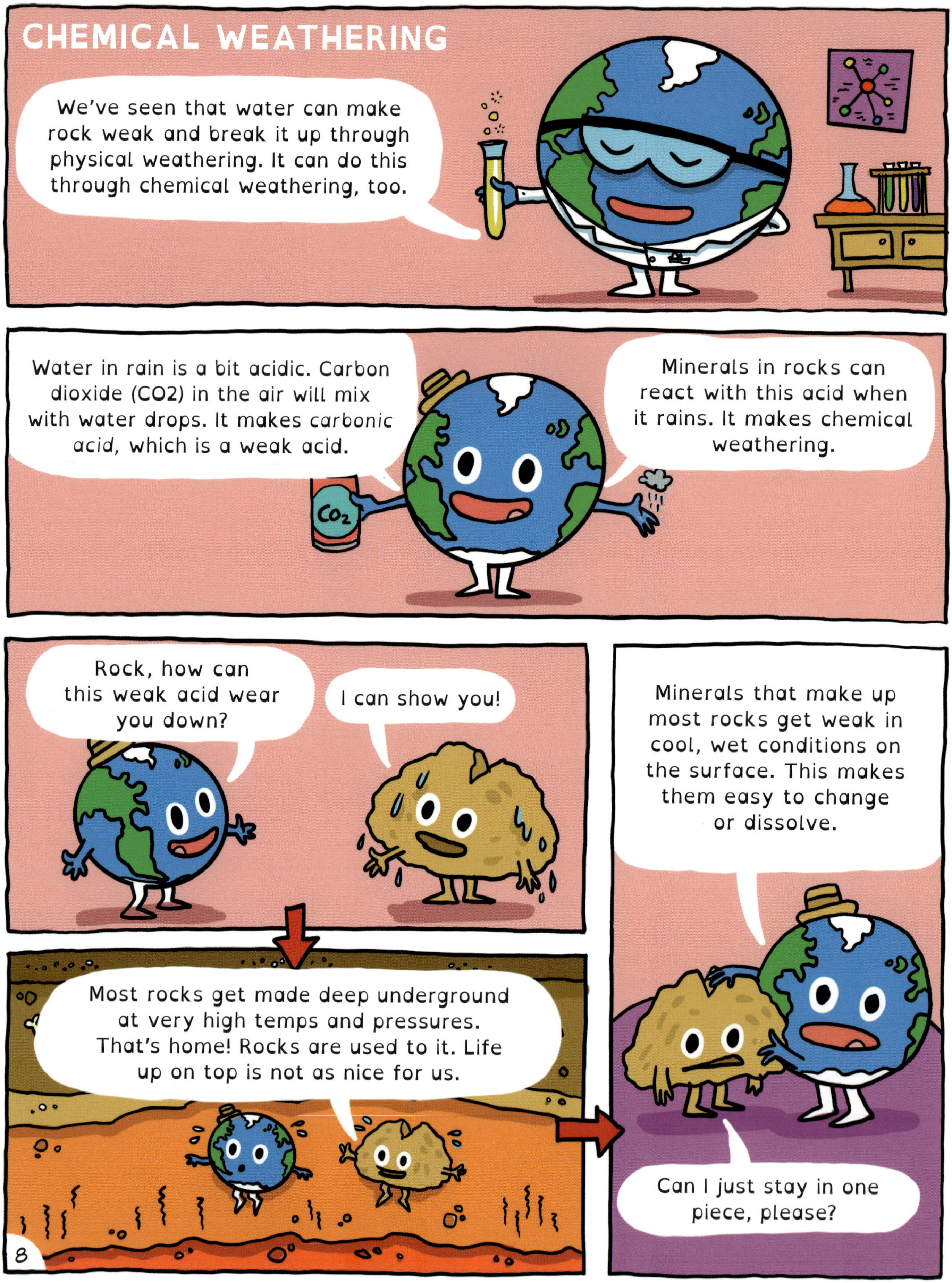
CHEMICAL WEATHERING
We've seen that water can make rock weak and break it up through physical weathering. It can do this through chemical weathering, too.
Water in rain is a bit acidic. Carbon dioxide (CO2) in the air will mix with water drops. It makes *carbonic acid,* which is a weak acid.
CO2
Minerals in rocks can react with this acid when it rains. It makes chemical weathering.
Rock, how can this weak acid wear you down?
I can show you!
Most rocks get made deep underground at very high temps and pressures. That's home! Rocks are used to it. Life up on top is not as nice for us.
Minerals that make up most rocks get weak in cool, wet conditions on the surface. This makes them easy to change or dissolve.
Can I just stay in one piece, please?

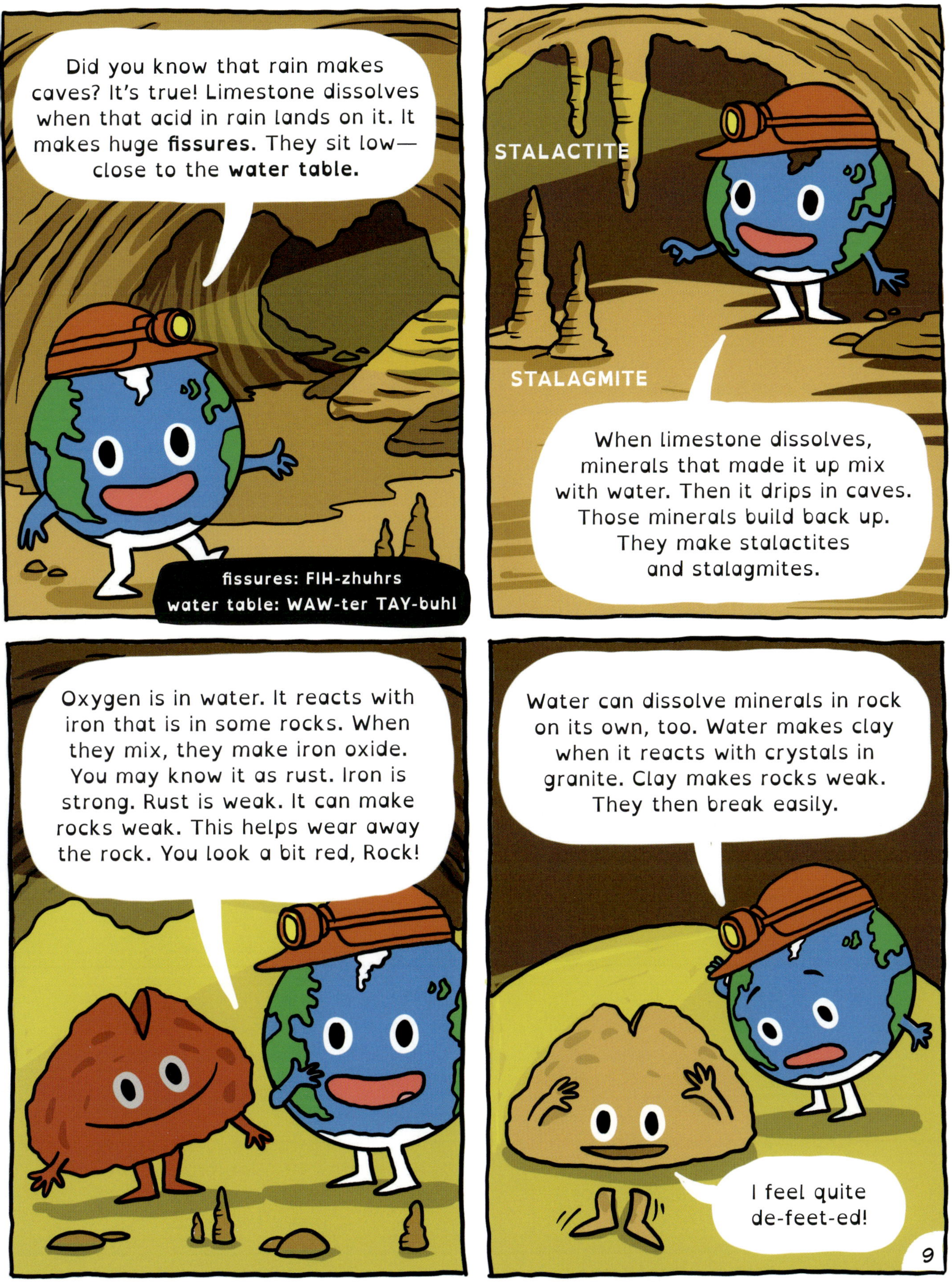
Did you know that rain makes caves? It's true! Limestone dissolves when that acid in rain lands on it. It makes huge **fissures.** They sit low—close to the **water table.**
fissures: FIH-zhuhrs
water table: WAW-ter TAY-buhl
STALACTITE
STALAGMITE
When limestone dissolves, minerals that made it up mix with water. Then it drips in caves. Those minerals build back up. They make stalactites and stalagmites.
Oxygen is in water. It reacts with iron that is in some rocks. When they mix, they make iron oxide. You may know it as rust. Iron is strong. Rust is weak. It can make rocks weak. This helps wear away the rock. You look a bit red, Rock!
Water can dissolve minerals in rock on its own, too. Water makes clay when it reacts with crystals in granite. Clay makes rocks weak. They then break easily.
I feel quite de-feet-ed!

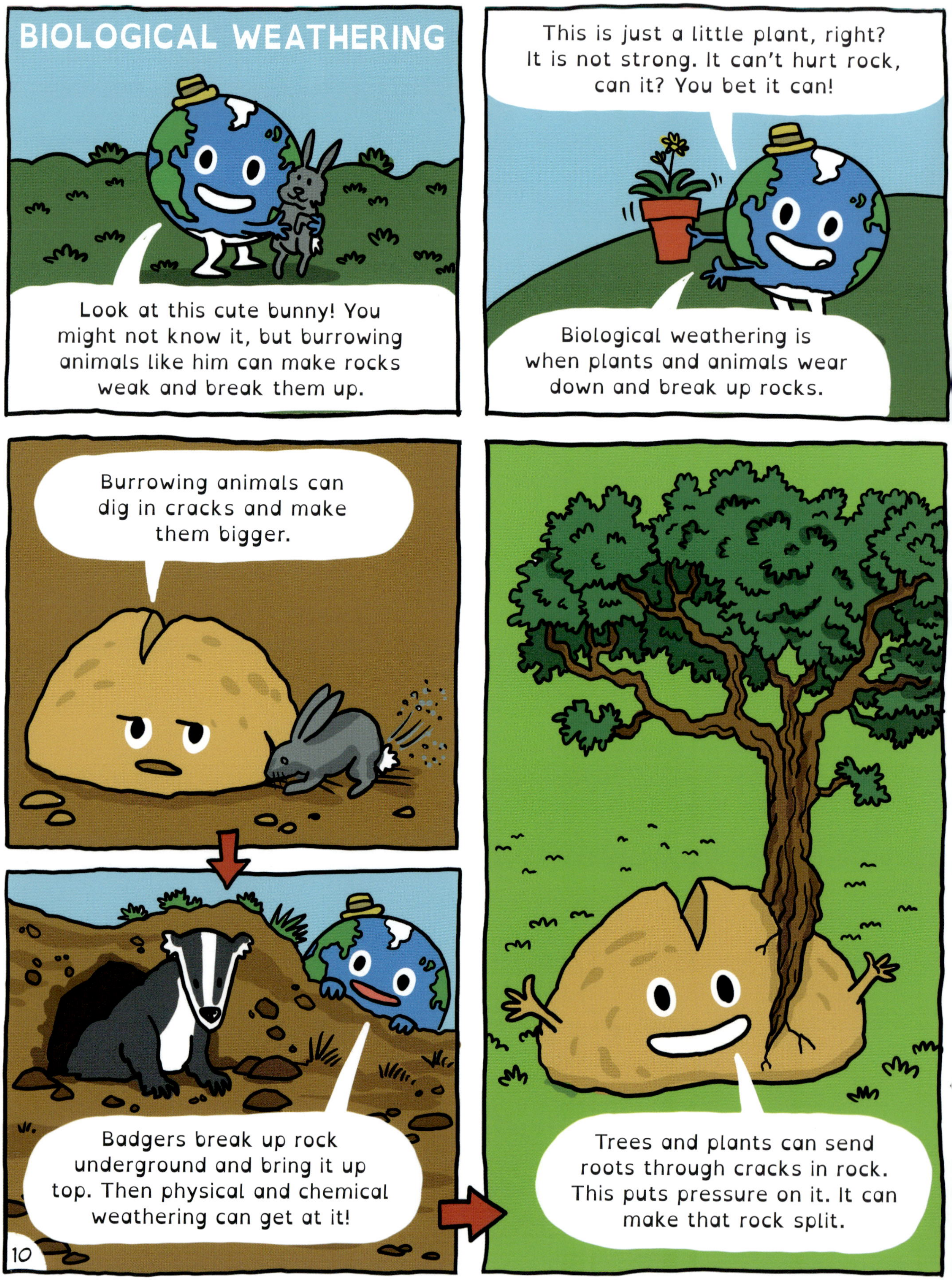
BIOLOGICAL WEATHERING
Look at this cute bunny! You might not know it, but burrowing animals like him can make rocks weak and break them up.
This is just a little plant, right? It is not strong. It can't hurt rock, can it? You bet it can!
Biological weathering is when plants and animals wear down and break up rocks.
Burrowing animals can dig in cracks and make them bigger.
Badgers break up rock underground and bring it up top. Then physical and chemical weathering can get at it!
Trees and plants can send roots through cracks in rock. This puts pressure on it. It can make that rock split.

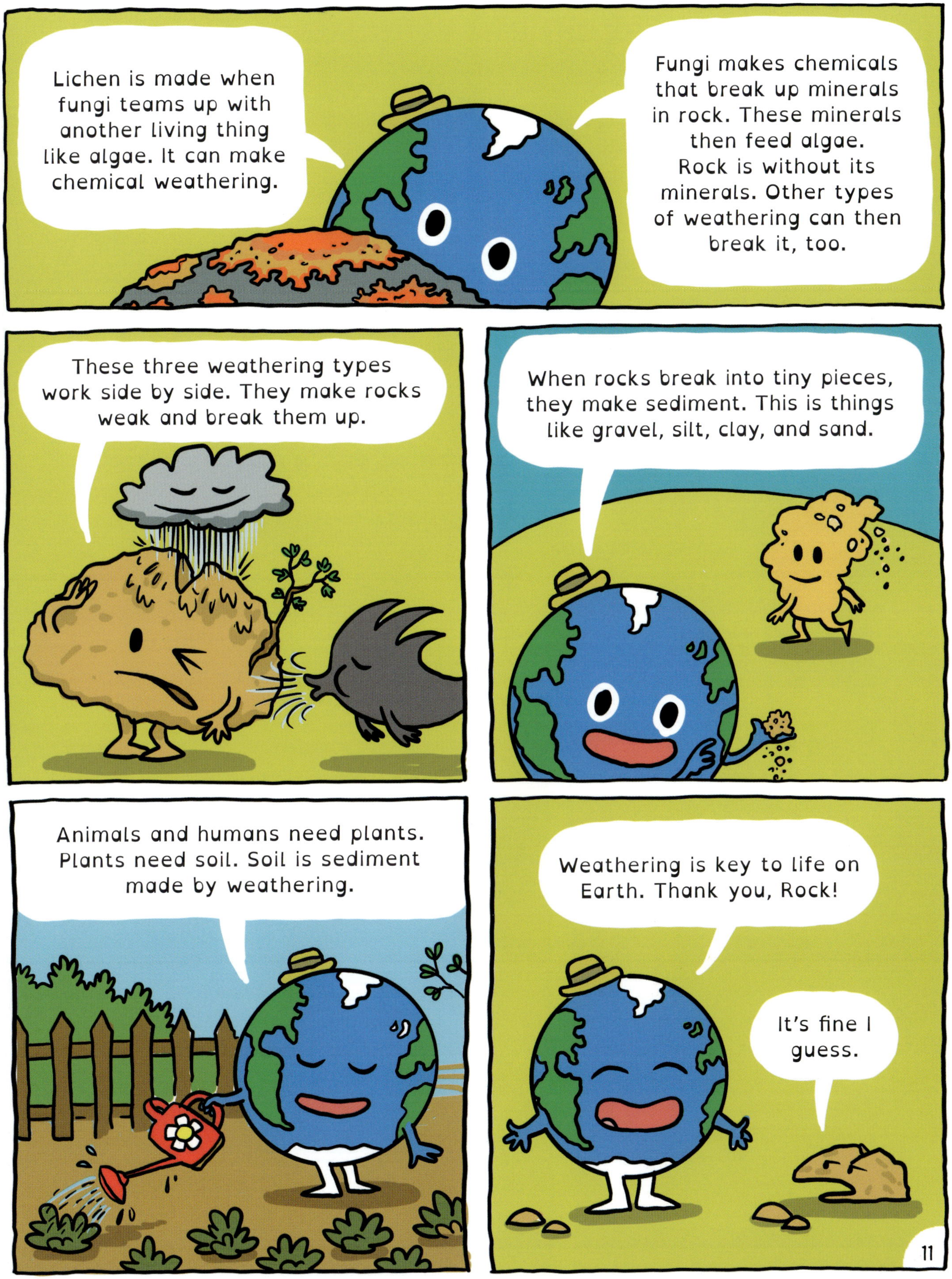
Lichen is made when fungi teams up with another living thing like algae. It can make chemical weathering.
Fungi makes chemicals that break up minerals in rock. These minerals then feed algae. Rock is without its minerals. Other types of weathering can then break it, too.
These three weathering types work side by side. They make rocks weak and break them up.
When rocks break into tiny pieces, they make sediment. This is things like gravel, silt, clay, and sand.
Animals and humans need plants. Plants need soil. Soil is sediment made by weathering.
Weathering is key to life on Earth. Thank you, Rock!
It's fine I guess.

ERROSION AND DEPOSITION

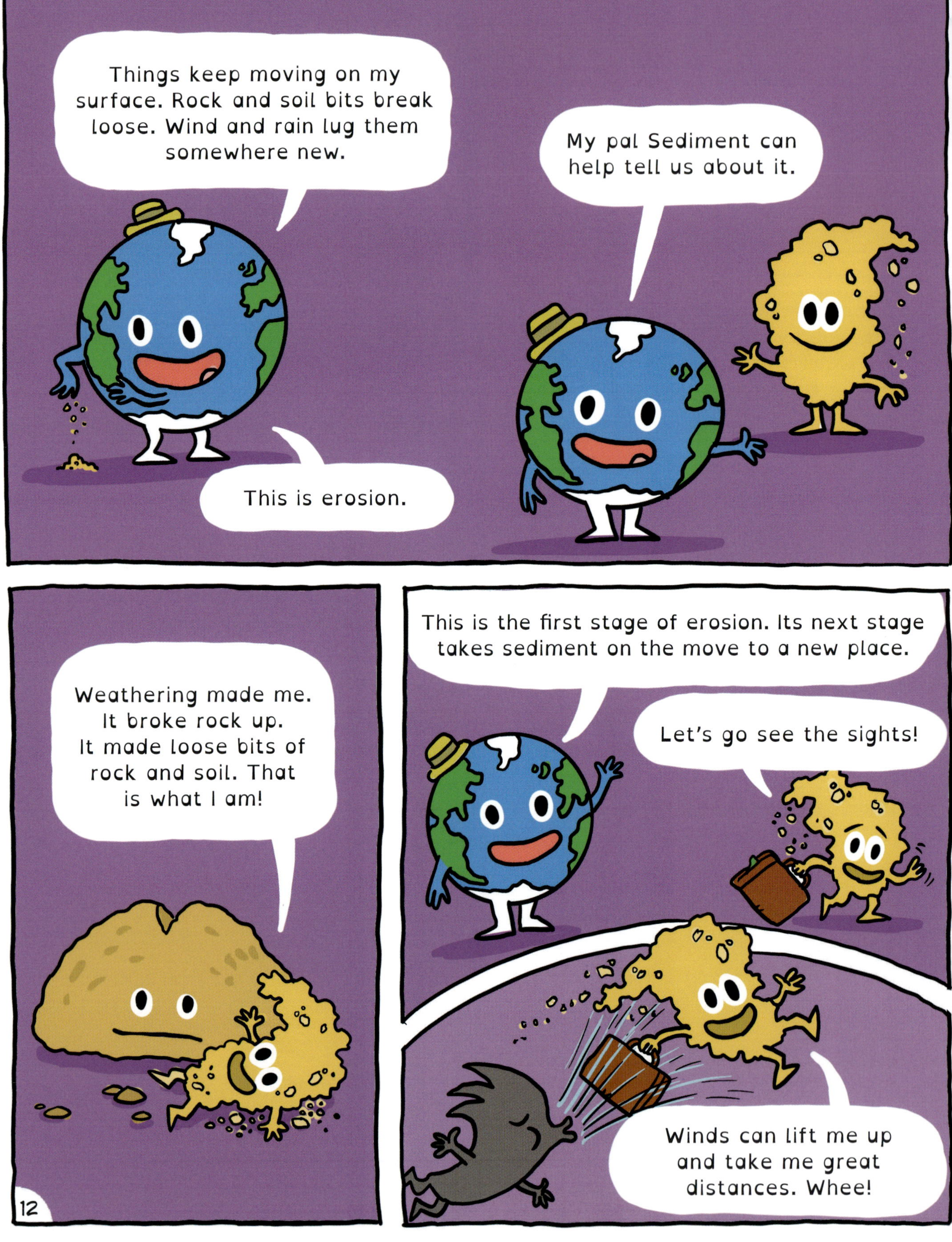
Things keep moving on my surface. Rock and soil bits break loose. Wind and rain lug them somewhere new.
This is erosion.
My pal Sediment can help tell us about it.
Weathering made me. It broke rock up. It made loose bits of rock and soil. That is what I am!
This is the first stage of erosion. Its next stage takes sediment on the move to a new place.
Let's go see the sights!
Winds can lift me up and take me great distances. Whee!

Rain can drop me in rivers and streams. Glug!
This trip ends when I am built up on land. This is deposition.
I might end up as this desert sand dune...
...or this river bed.
Can you wait millions of years? Pressure and time might make me **sedimentary rock.**
sedimentary rock: sed-uh-MEN-tuh-ree ROK

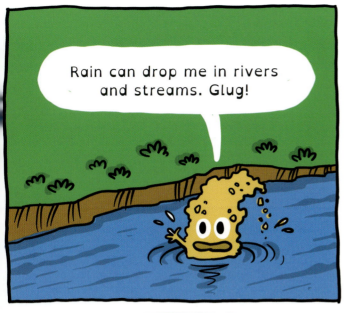

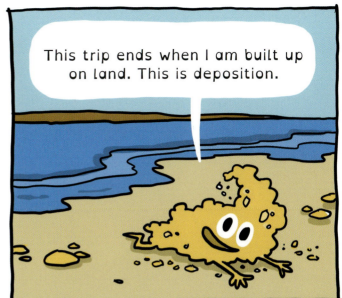

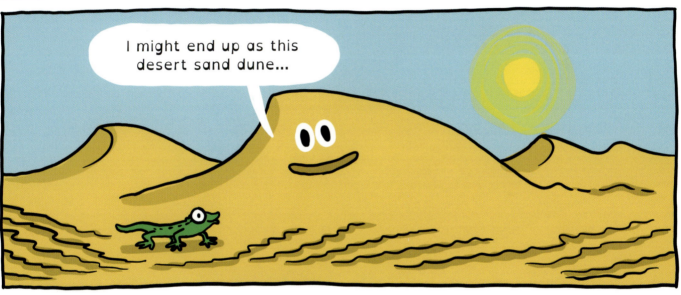

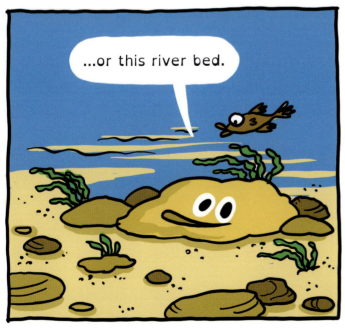

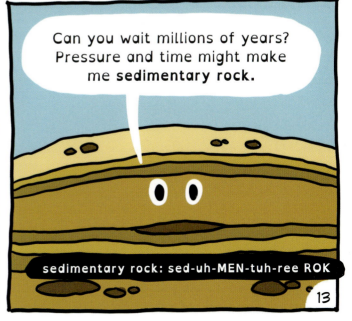

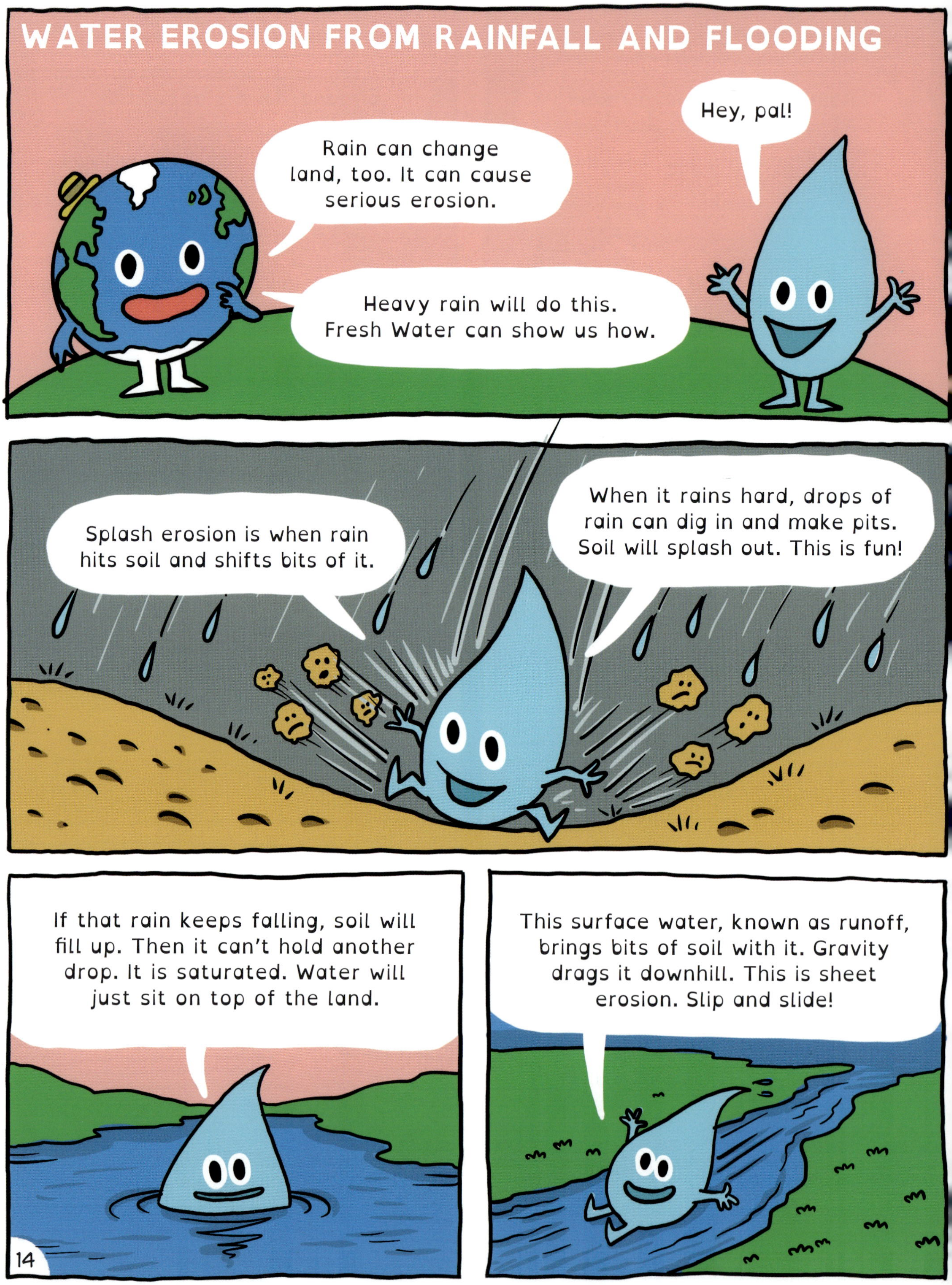
WATER EROSION FROM RAINFALL AND FLOODING
Rain can change land, too. It can cause serious erosion.
Heavy rain will do this. Fresh Water can show us how.
Hey, pal!
Splash erosion is when rain hits soil and shifts bits of it.
When it rains hard, drops of rain can dig in and make pits. Soil will splash out. This is fun!
If that rain keeps falling, soil will fill up. Then it can't hold another drop. It is saturated. Water will just sit on top of the land.
This surface water, known as runoff, brings bits of soil with it. Gravity drags it downhill. This is sheet erosion. Slip and slide!

As it flows, water will dig small grooves in the soil known as rills. Water flows fast through rills. It can make more soil loose and take those bits with it, too.
Strong rain and melting snow can make lots of runoff. Then rills can get deep. They may make gullies. These are bigger and deeper. More land is eroded.
Look how I shape this land!
This rain will not stop!
Heavy rains and storms can make flash floods. Flash floods erode soil fast.
Erosion like this can wreck farms if it sweeps off the soil's rich top layer.
It can make badlands, too. This is a place with small, steep hills and deep gullies. You can find them in dry spots like deserts. They have thin soil and few plants.

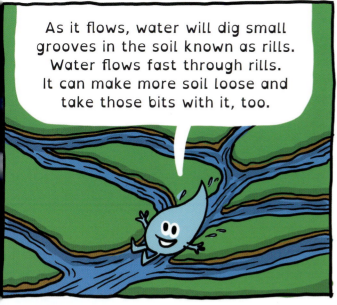

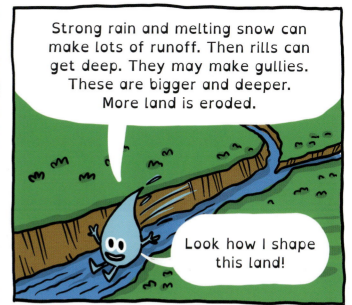

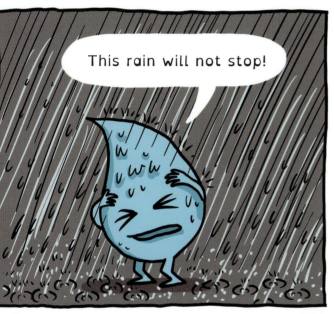

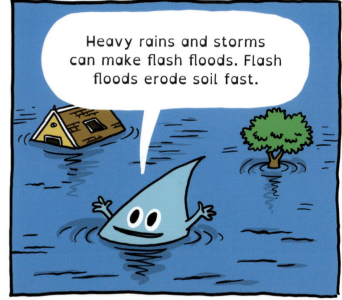

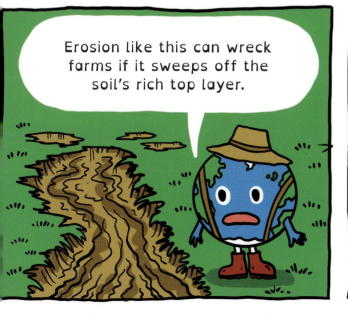

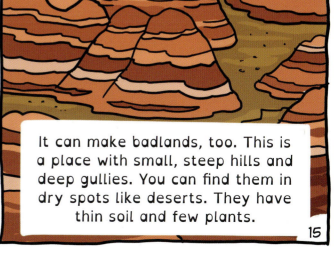

WATER EROSION FROM RIVERS
Lots of land is eroded when rivers flow through it. Sediment is back to tell us more.
Hello again! When I am in a river, I am known as its **load.** You can find me in three forms.
load: LOHD
In this form, I am too small to see. I am microscopic. I am dissolved in the water. Like this, I am known as a dissolved load.
I can get a bit bigger like this. This is when clay, silt, and sand float along in rivers. Like this, I am known as a suspended load.
Last but not least, like this I am a bed load. These bits are too big. They weigh too much. They can't float. They bump along the river bed. As they bump, they can knock rocks and soil loose, eroding the river bed.
Rivers have stages. Erosion looks different at each stage.

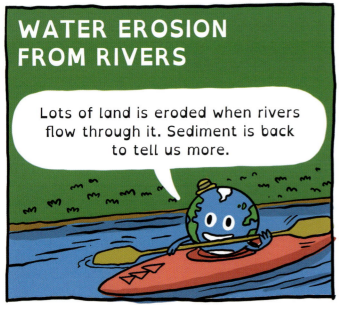

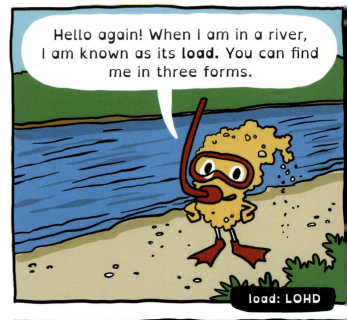

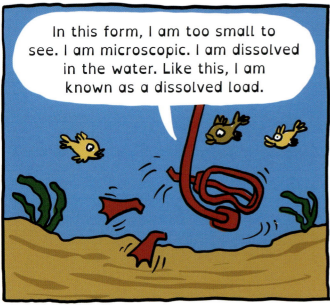

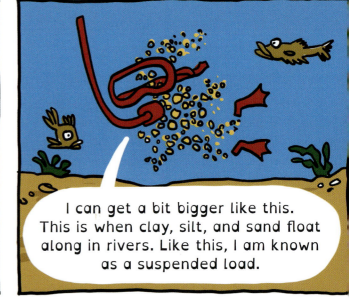

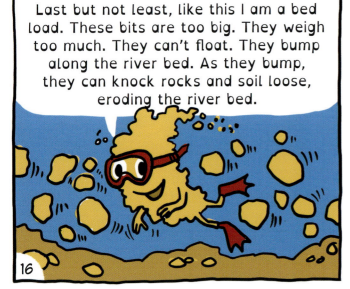

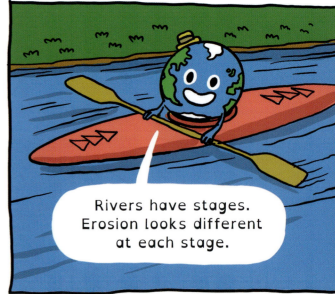

Hey, this is fast! Rivers start up on high land like in mountains. Land's **gradient** is its slope. In this place, its slope is steep. Water flows fast. It digs up land and cuts a deep, V-shaped channel.

gradient: GRAY-dee-uhnt

Look at this bend!

As rivers flow lower, land is less steep. The rivers slow. They may wind back and forth on the land. These bends are known as meanders. At this stage, each river erodes less bits of land from its bed and more from its sides.

As rivers flow through flat land, they slow right up. They erode outer **banks.** Then they drop those land bits on inner banks. That makes this shape. It looks like a snake.

banks: BANGX

When rivers flood, they drop sediment. This makes flat *flood plains* when floods end. Soil in this place is rich and helps crops grow well.

Looks like this trip ends here!

Rivers flow into larger bodies of water, such as bays, gulfs, and seas. The place they meet is the river's mouth. It might get wide in this place.

At its end, it slows. It drops its sediment. This may build up. It can make a plain with three sides known as a delta. These plains have rich soil that can help crops grow well.

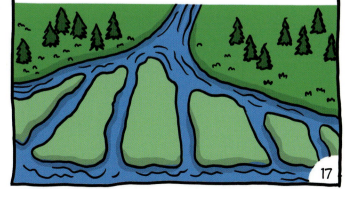

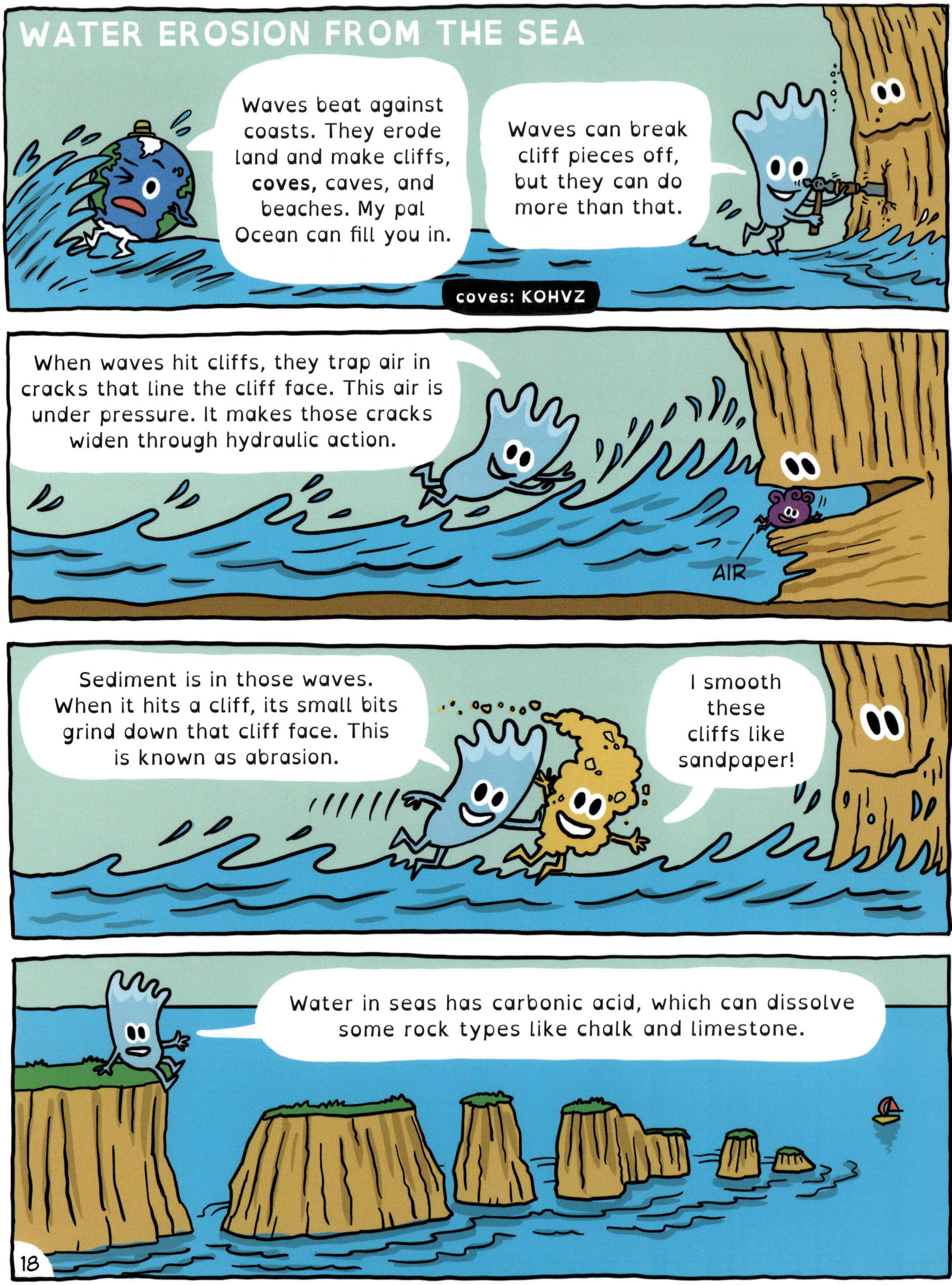
WATER EROSION FROM THE SEA
Waves beat against coasts. They erode land and make cliffs, **coves,** caves, and beaches. My pal Ocean can fill you in.
Waves can break cliff pieces off, but they can do more than that.
coves: KOHVZ
When waves hit cliffs, they trap air in cracks that line the cliff face. This air is under pressure. It makes those cracks widen through hydraulic action.
AIR
Sediment is in those waves. When it hits a cliff, its small bits grind down that cliff face. This is known as abrasion.
I smooth these cliffs like sandpaper!
Water in seas has carbonic acid, which can dissolve some rock types like chalk and limestone.

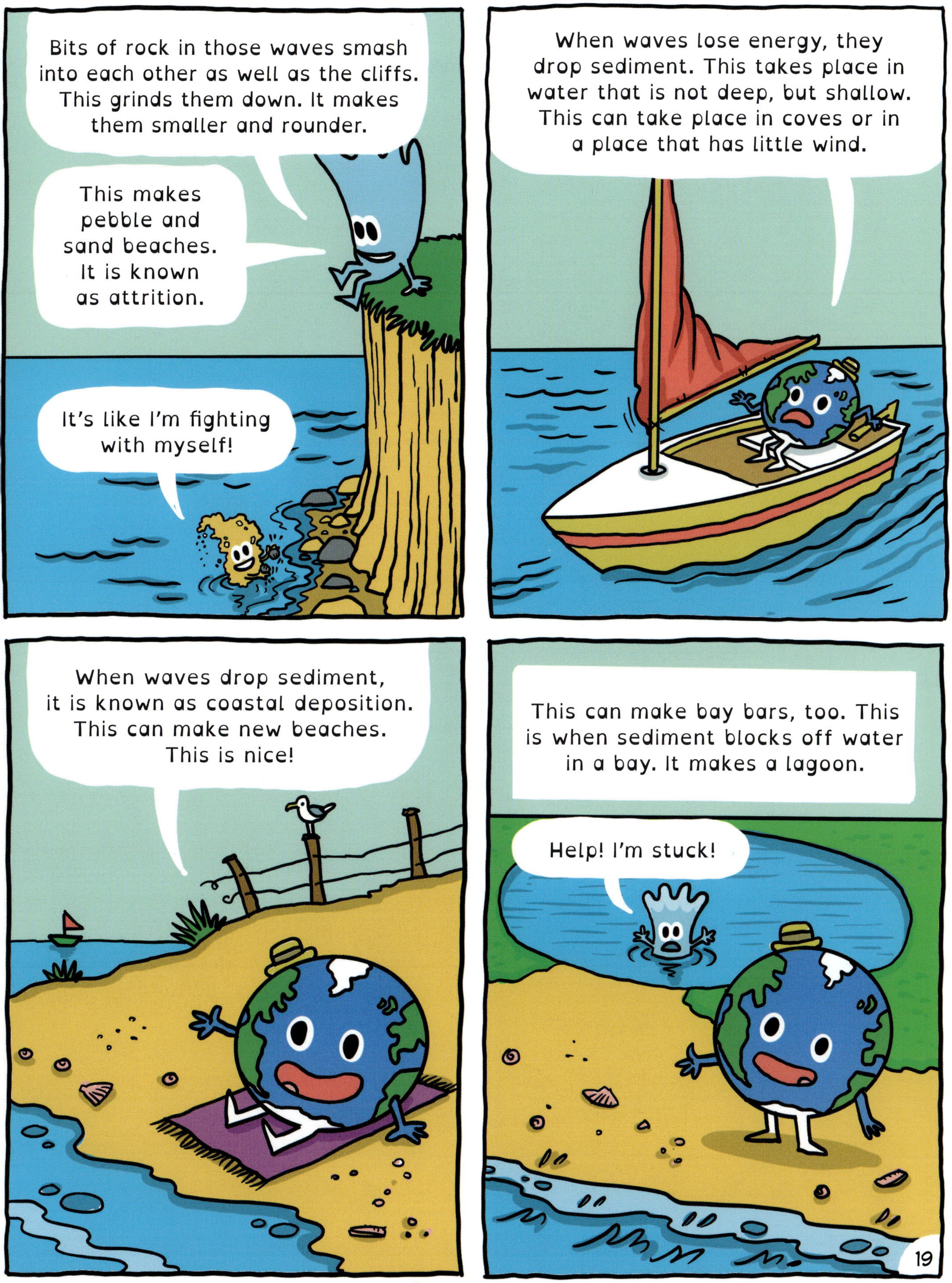
Bits of rock in those waves smash into each other as well as the cliffs. This grinds them down. It makes them smaller and rounder.
This makes pebble and sand beaches. It is known as attrition.
It's like I'm fighting with myself!
When waves lose energy, they drop sediment. This takes place in water that is not deep, but shallow. This can take place in coves or in a place that has little wind.
When waves drop sediment, it is known as coastal deposition. This can make new beaches. This is nice!
This can make bay bars, too. This is when sediment blocks off water in a bay. It makes a lagoon.
Help! I'm stuck!

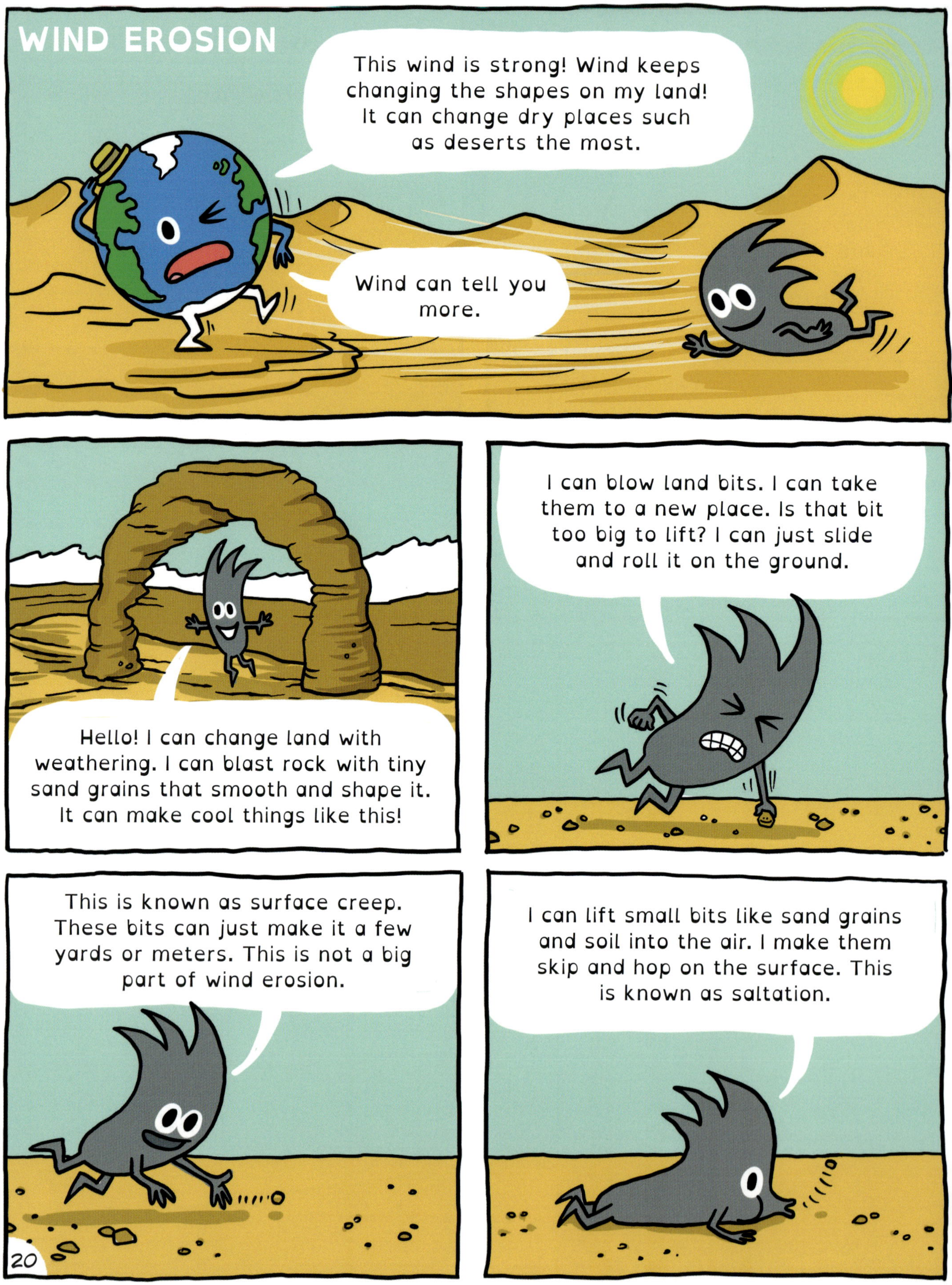
WIND EROSION
This wind is strong! Wind keeps changing the shapes on my land! It can change dry places such as deserts the most.
Wind can tell you more.
Hello! I can change land with weathering. I can blast rock with tiny sand grains that smooth and shape it. It can make cool things like this!
I can blow land bits. I can take them to a new place. Is that bit too big to lift? I can just slide and roll it on the ground.
This is known as surface creep. These bits can just make it a few yards or meters. This is not a big part of wind erosion.
I can lift small bits like sand grains and soil into the air. I make them skip and hop on the surface. This is known as saltation.

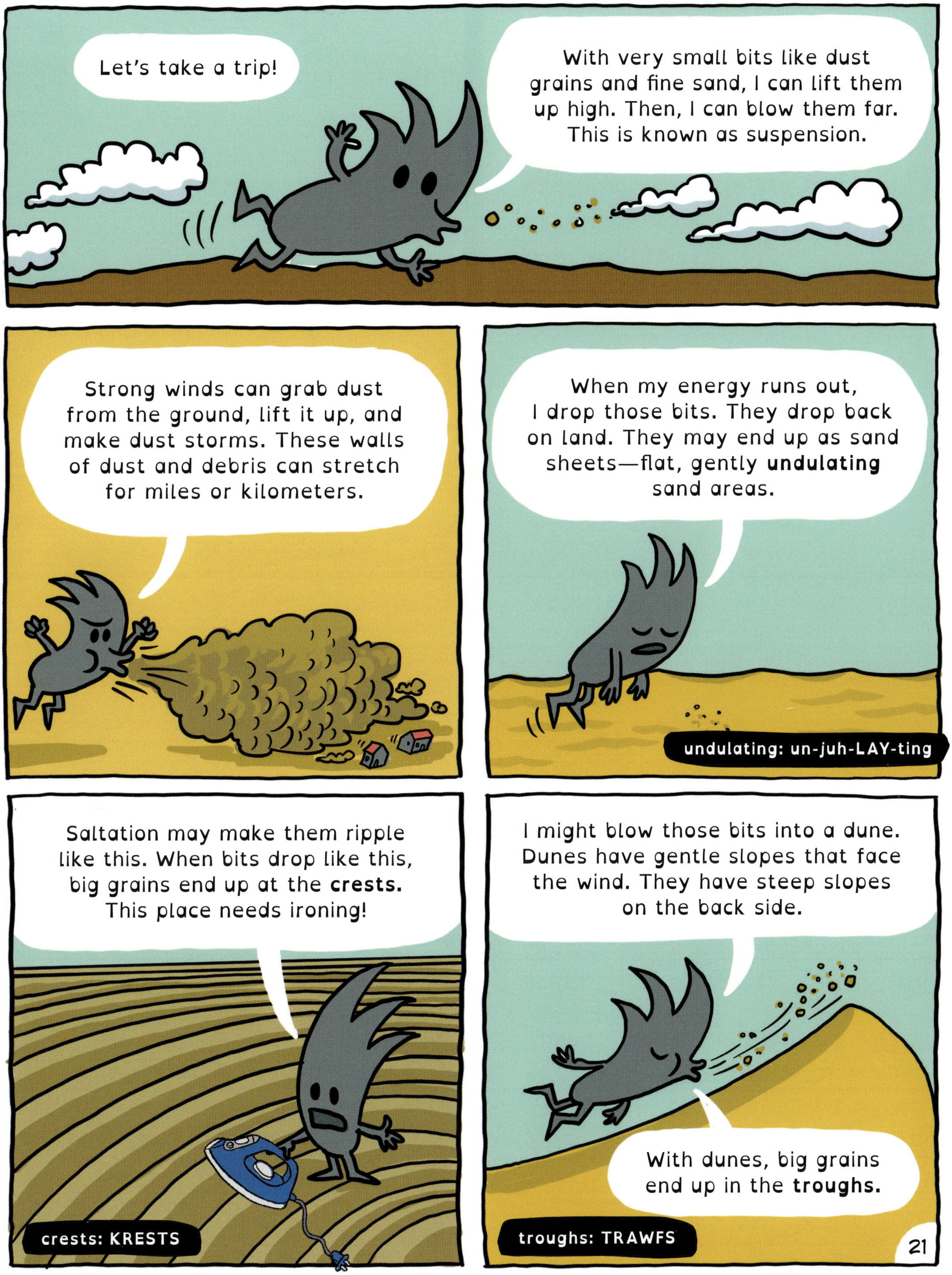
Let's take a trip!
With very small bits like dust grains and fine sand, I can lift them up high. Then, I can blow them far. This is known as suspension.
Strong winds can grab dust from the ground, lift it up, and make dust storms. These walls of dust and debris can stretch for miles or kilometers.
When my energy runs out, I drop those bits. They drop back on land. They may end up as sand sheets—flat, gently **undulating** sand areas.
undulating: un-juh-LAY-ting
Saltation may make them ripple like this. When bits drop like this, big grains end up at the **crests.** This place needs ironing!
crests: KRESTS
I might blow those bits into a dune. Dunes have gentle slopes that face the wind. They have steep slopes on the back side.
With dunes, big grains end up in the **troughs.**
troughs: TRAWFS

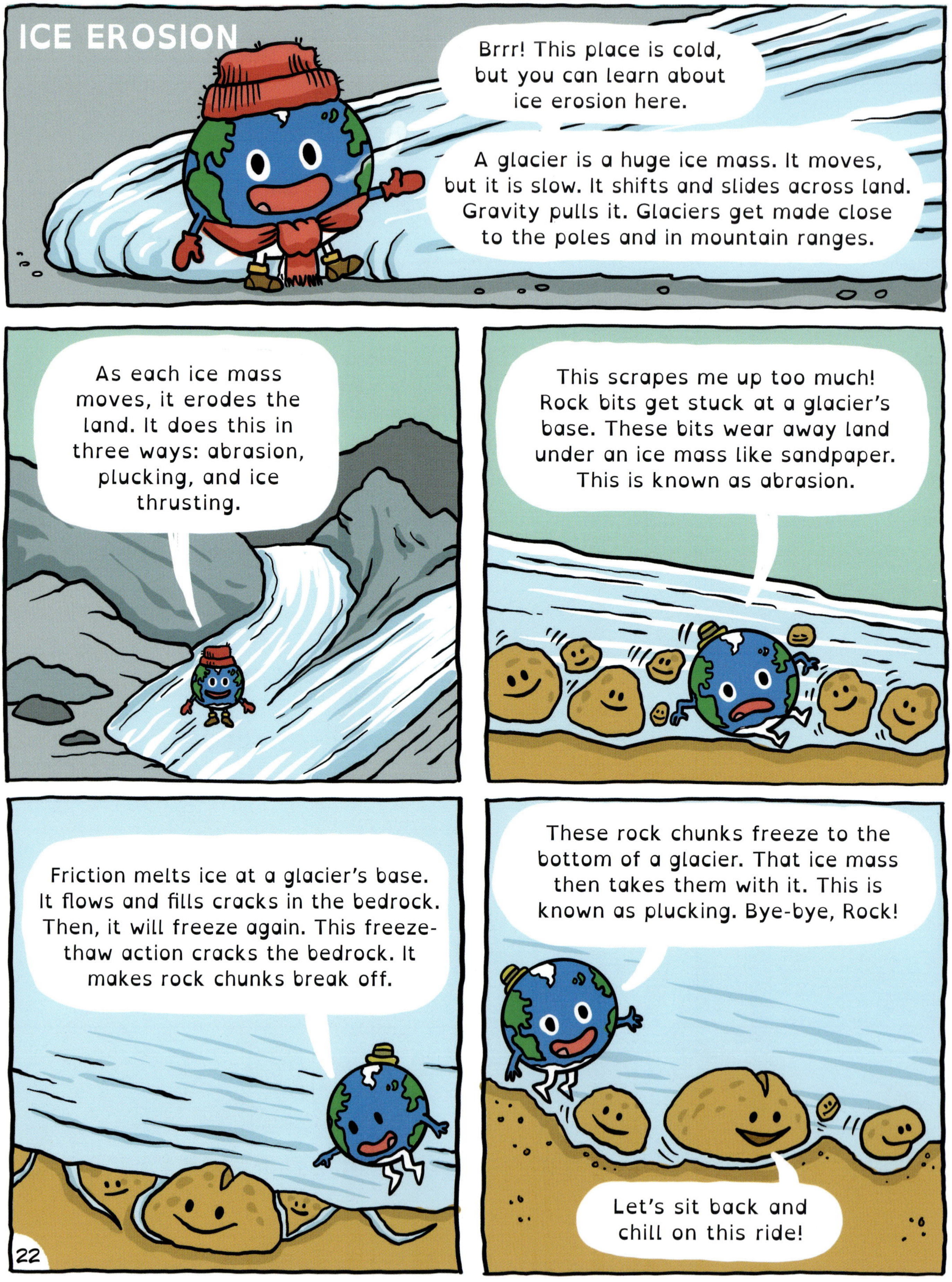
ICE EROSION
Brrr! This place is cold, but you can learn about ice erosion here.
A glacier is a huge ice mass. It moves, but it is slow. It shifts and slides across land. Gravity pulls it. Glaciers get made close to the poles and in mountain ranges.
As each ice mass moves, it erodes the land. It does this in three ways: abrasion, plucking, and ice thrusting.
This scrapes me up too much! Rock bits get stuck at a glacier's base. These bits wear away land under an ice mass like sandpaper. This is known as abrasion.
Friction melts ice at a glacier's base. It flows and fills cracks in the bedrock. Then, it will freeze again. This freeze-thaw action cracks the bedrock. It makes rock chunks break off.
These rock chunks freeze to the bottom of a glacier. That ice mass then takes them with it. This is known as plucking. Bye-bye, Rock!
Let's sit back and chill on this ride!

A glacier may freeze to land it is on top of. Then, it leaps forward. Huge sediment sheets stay frozen to it when it breaks free. This is known as ice thrusting. This has made many lake basins.
Hey!
LATERAL MORAINE
MEDIAL MORAINE
A moraine is made when a glacier drops things as it moves. It leaves bands of debris on each side as it goes through a mountain valley. These are known as lateral moraines.
If 2 glaciers meet and join up, these lateral moraines that run between them make this medial moraine.
When temps rise, a glacier stops. It melts. As it melts, it drops debris, which builds up. It makes a ridge like this. This ridge makes a terminal moraine.
It looks like this trip is at its end!
Before a glacier slides through, most mountain valleys have a V shape. Mountain streams make that shape as they pass.
Glaciers cut through land. They will widen, deepen, and smooth valleys. They leave them in U shapes. Like I told you, glaciers change the land!

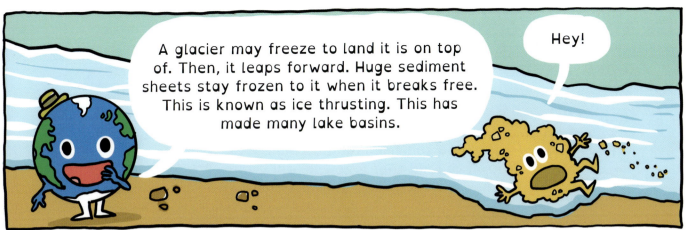

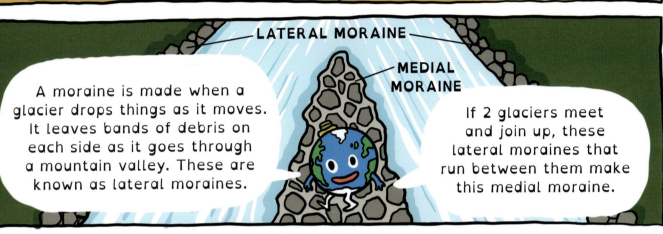

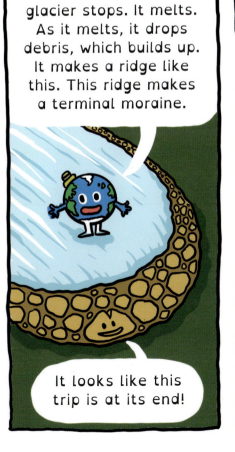

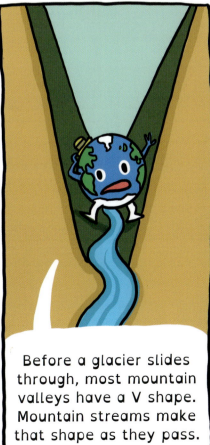

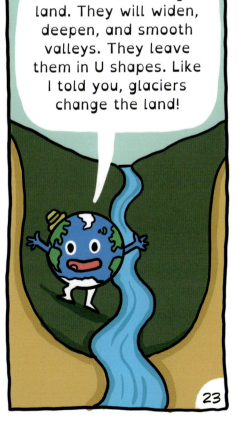

GRAVITY EROSION

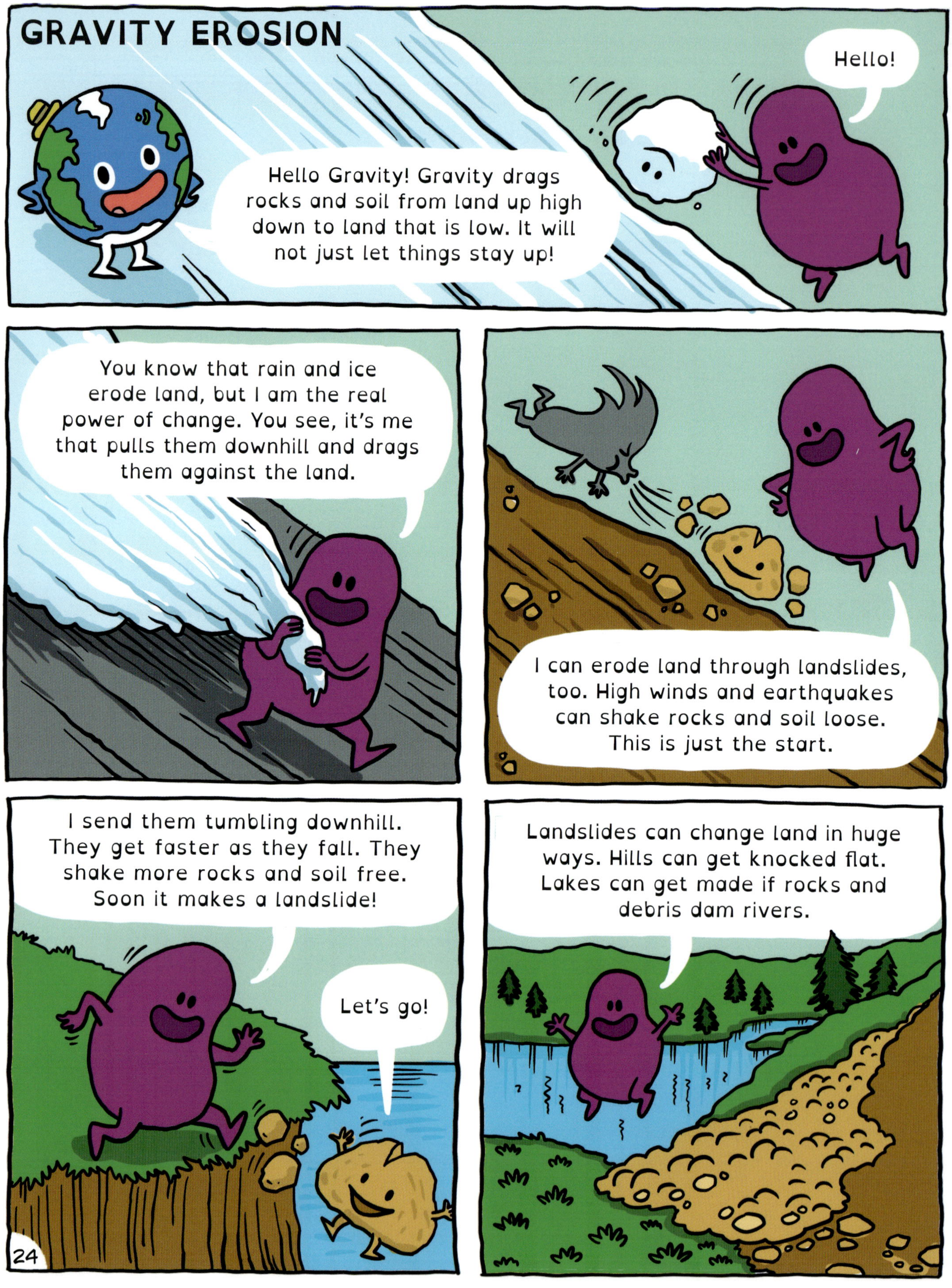
Hello!
Hello Gravity! Gravity drags rocks and soil from land up high down to land that is low. It will not just let things stay up!
You know that rain and ice erode land, but I am the real power of change. You see, it's me that pulls them downhill and drags them against the land.
I can erode land through landslides, too. High winds and earthquakes can shake rocks and soil loose. This is just the start.
I send them tumbling downhill. They get faster as they fall. They shake more rocks and soil free. Soon it makes a landslide!
Let's go!
Landslides can change land in huge ways. Hills can get knocked flat. Lakes can get made if rocks and debris dam rivers.

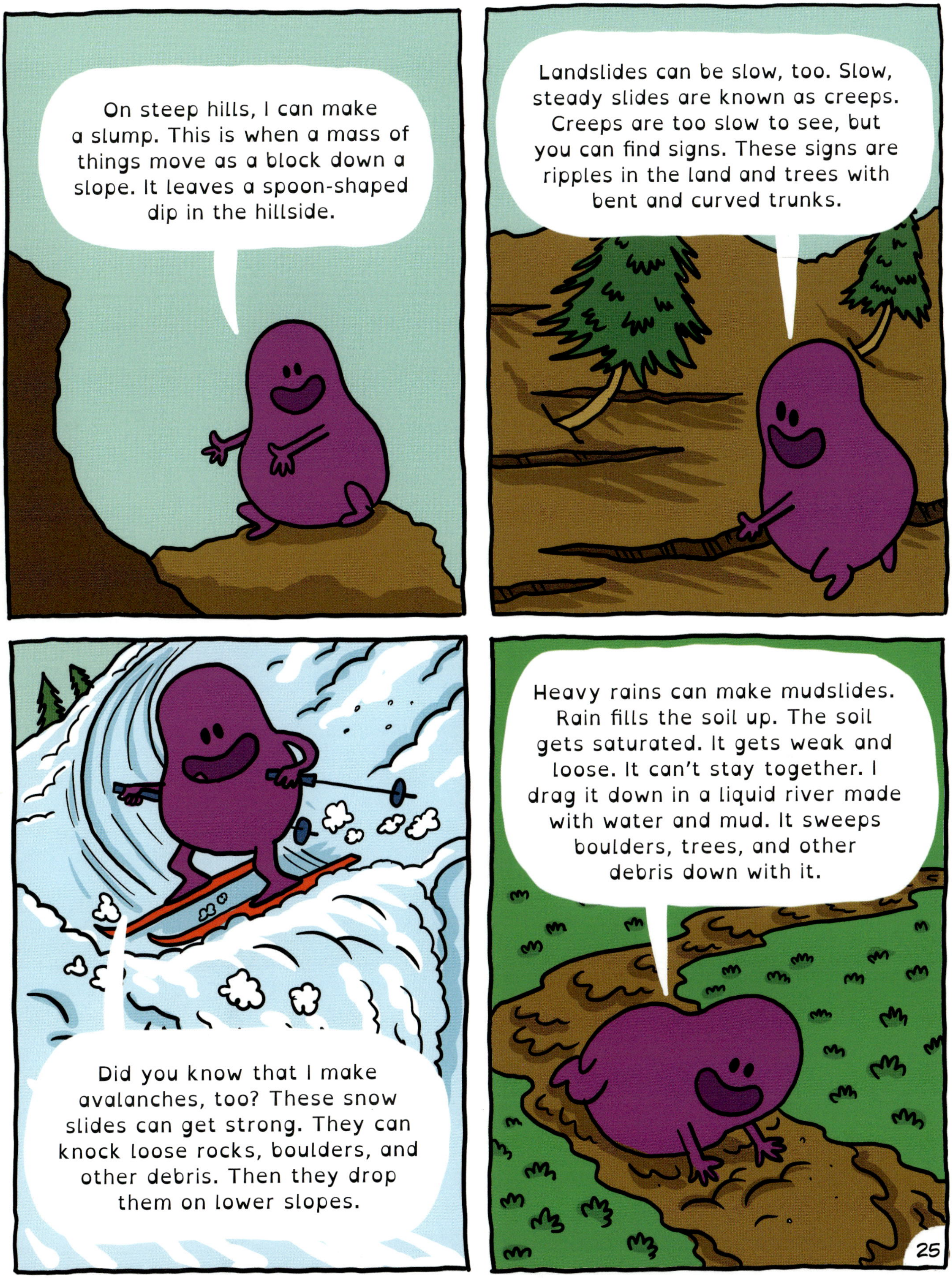
On steep hills, I can make a slump. This is when a mass of things move as a block down a slope. It leaves a spoon-shaped dip in the hillside.
Landslides can be slow, too. Slow, steady slides are known as creeps. Creeps are too slow to see, but you can find signs. These signs are ripples in the land and trees with bent and curved trunks.
Did you know that I make avalanches, too? These snow slides can get strong. They can knock loose rocks, boulders, and other debris. Then they drop them on lower slopes.
Heavy rains can make mudslides. Rain fills the soil up. The soil gets saturated. It gets weak and loose. It can't stay together. I drag it down in a liquid river made with water and mud. It sweeps boulders, trees, and other debris down with it.

INTERNAL PROCESSES
Now you know how surface forces change land. But take a look deep underground and you will see stuff at work that can change land in big ways.
Look at all these layers.
CONTINENTAL CRUST
OCEANIC
LITHOSPHERE
MANTLE
OUTER CORE
INNER CORE
ASTHENOSPHERE
I told you that this top crust is made up of plates. These **"tectonic plates"** shift slowly on top of hot, soft rock in the upper mantle.
These plates bump, crash, and slide with each other where their ends, or boundaries, meet.
tectonic plates: tek-TAH-nik PLAYTS
When plates shift away from each other, it is known as divergent boundaries. Magma, which is rock that is so hot it has melted (molten rock), will rise up and fill gaps left between plates. Magma then cools. It makes a hard new crust. This takes place the most on sea floors.
MAGMA

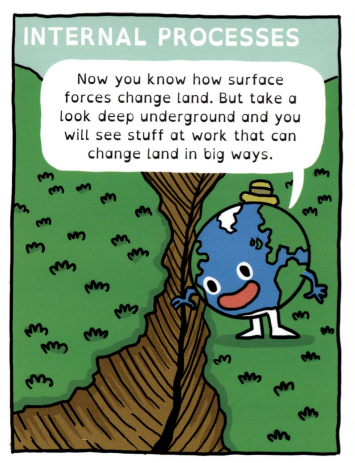

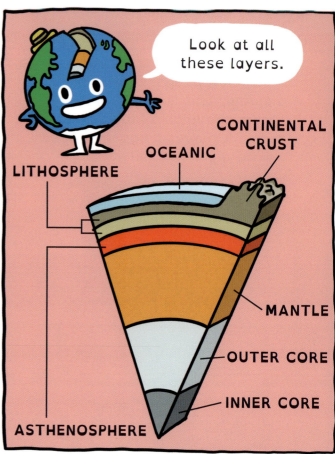

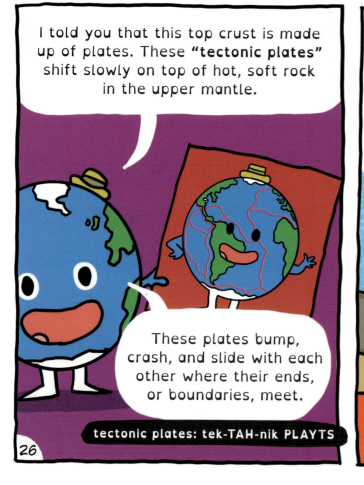

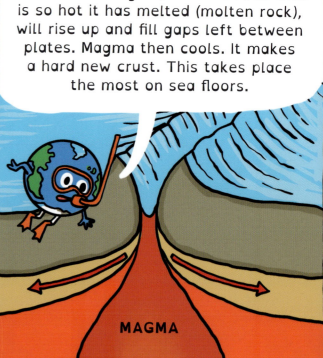

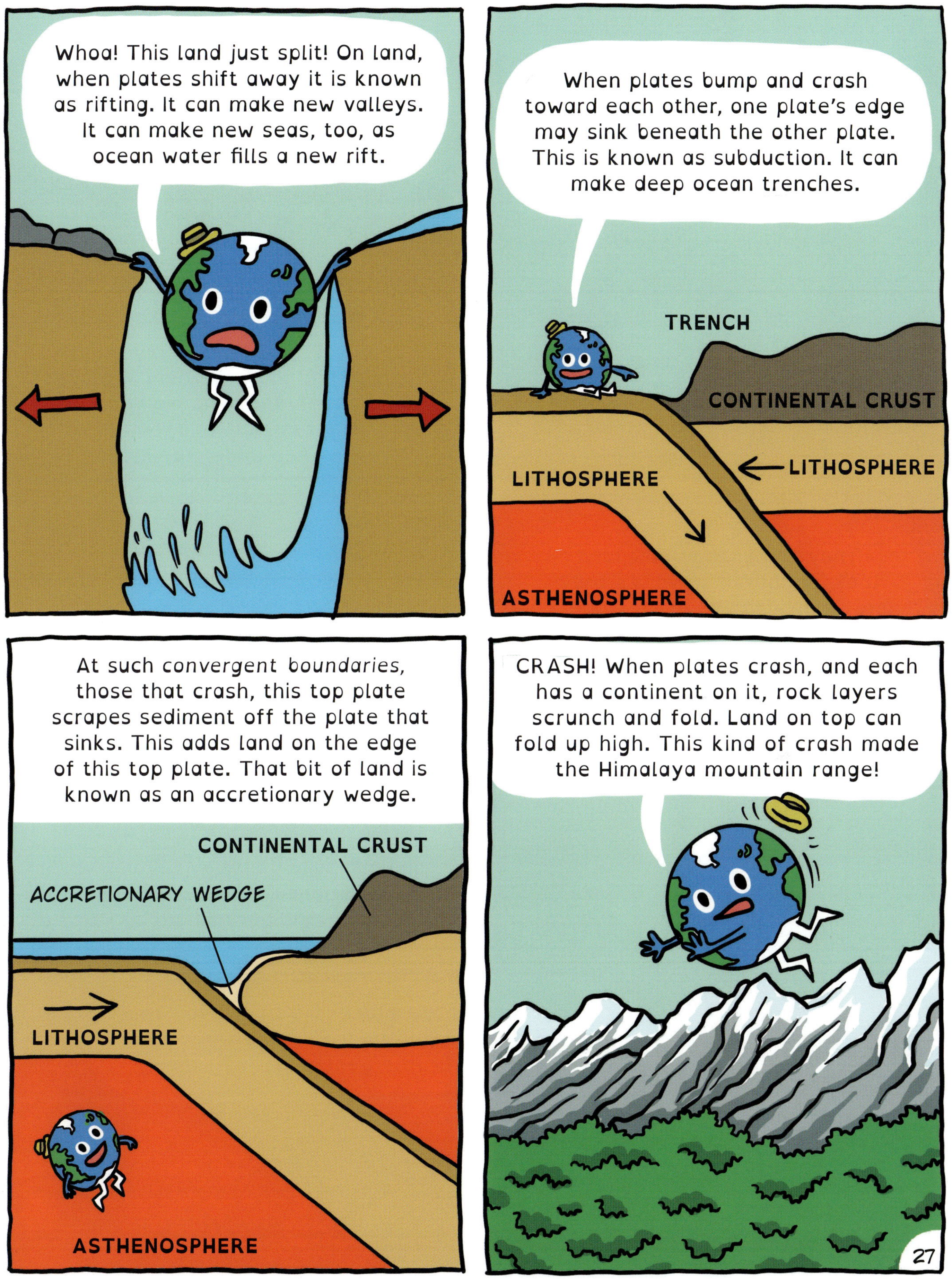
Whoa! This land just split! On land, when plates shift away it is known as rifting. It can make new valleys. It can make new seas, too, as ocean water fills a new rift.
When plates bump and crash toward each other, one plate's edge may sink beneath the other plate. This is known as subduction. It can make deep ocean trenches.
TRENCH
CONTINENTAL CRUST
LITHOSPHERE
LITHOSPHERE
ASTHENOSPHERE
At such *convergent boundaries,* those that crash, this top plate scrapes sediment off the plate that sinks. This adds land on the edge of this top plate. That bit of land is known as an accretionary wedge.
CONTINENTAL CRUST
ACCRETIONARY WEDGE
LITHOSPHERE
ASTHENOSPHERE
CRASH! When plates crash, and each has a continent on it, rock layers scrunch and fold. Land on top can fold up high. This kind of crash made the Himalaya mountain range!

VOLCANOES

Oops! When my guts mix and rage, huge, violent blasts can happen up on top, like a volcanic eruption.

Volcanoes are gaps in my crust. You can find most of them in places plates meet. Each is a big vent that lets out gases, ash, and molten rock from deep under the crust.

They can change how land looks in lots of ways. As they erupt, ash hills, **lava,** or cinders build up on the vent.

lava: LAH-vuh

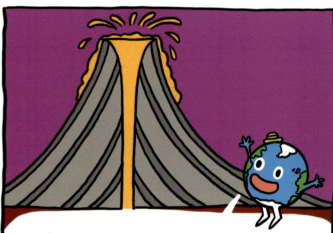

Look at you way up high! This tall cone is a stratovolcano. It is made when lava and ash build up. They build up when huge eruptions take place now and then for thousands or millions of years.

This wide and low place is a shield volcano. Its sides slope gently. It is made when thin, runny lava erupts gently lots of times.

Whoa! Did you see that? Lava blobs can shoot up high. They cool in the air. Then they drop as rock bits known as cinders.

These cinders pile up and make cinder cone volcanoes.

This vent grew big! See this bowl-shaped **crater**? It rings this vent. Its top might crash and sink after a huge volcanic eruption. This makes a big land dip known as a caldera. These can get huge!

crater: KRAY-tuhr

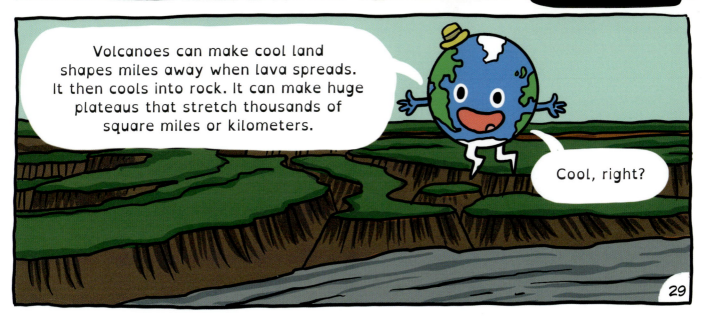

Volcanoes can make cool land shapes miles away when lava spreads. It then cools into rock. It can make huge plateaus that stretch thousands of square miles or kilometers.

Cool, right?

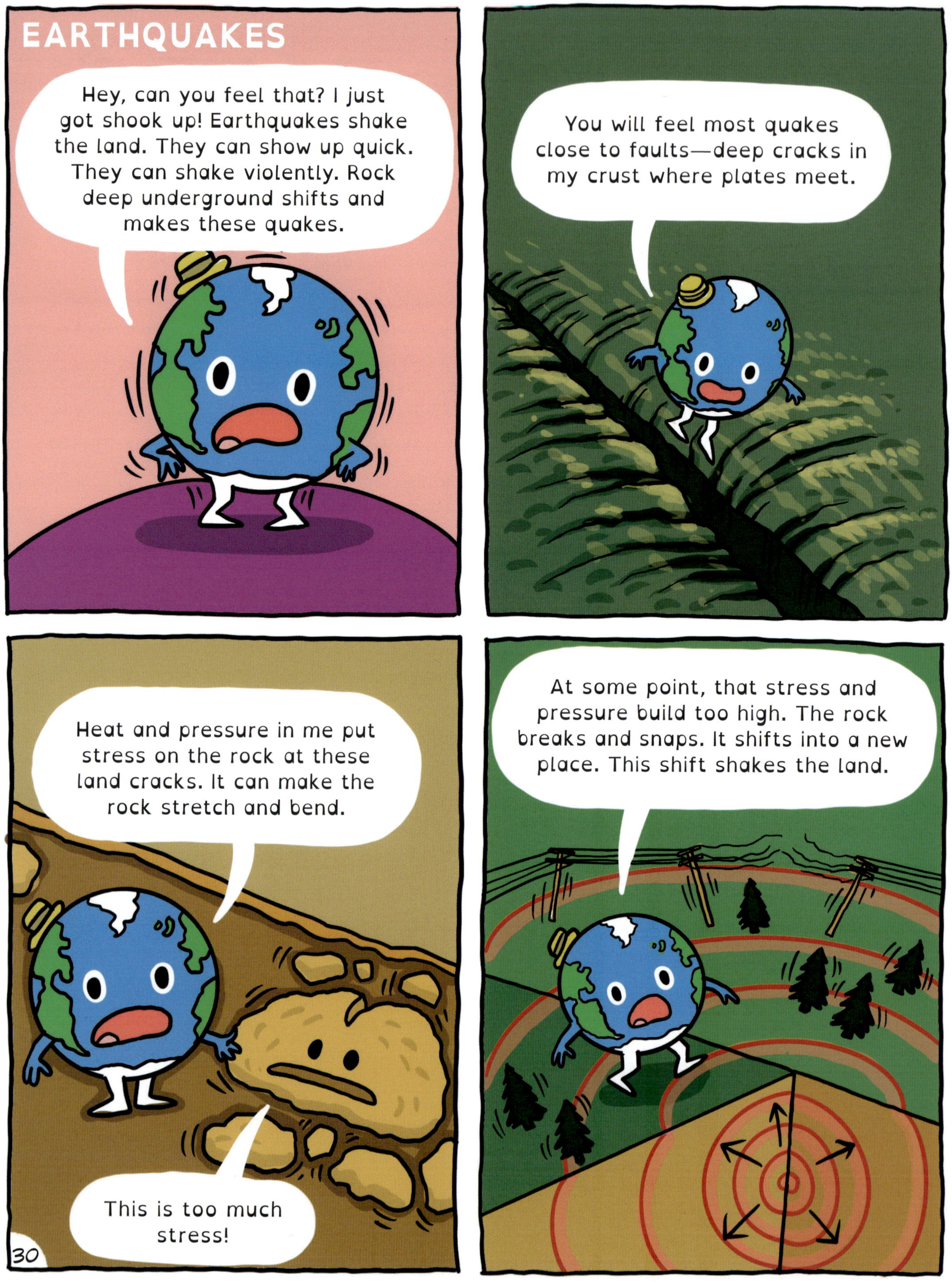
EARTHQUAKES
Hey, can you feel that? I just got shook up! Earthquakes shake the land. They can show up quick. They can shake violently. Rock deep underground shifts and makes these quakes.
You will feel most quakes close to faults—deep cracks in my crust where plates meet.
Heat and pressure in me put stress on the rock at these land cracks. It can make the rock stretch and bend.
This is too much stress!
At some point, that stress and pressure build too high. The rock breaks and snaps. It shifts into a new place. This shift shakes the land.

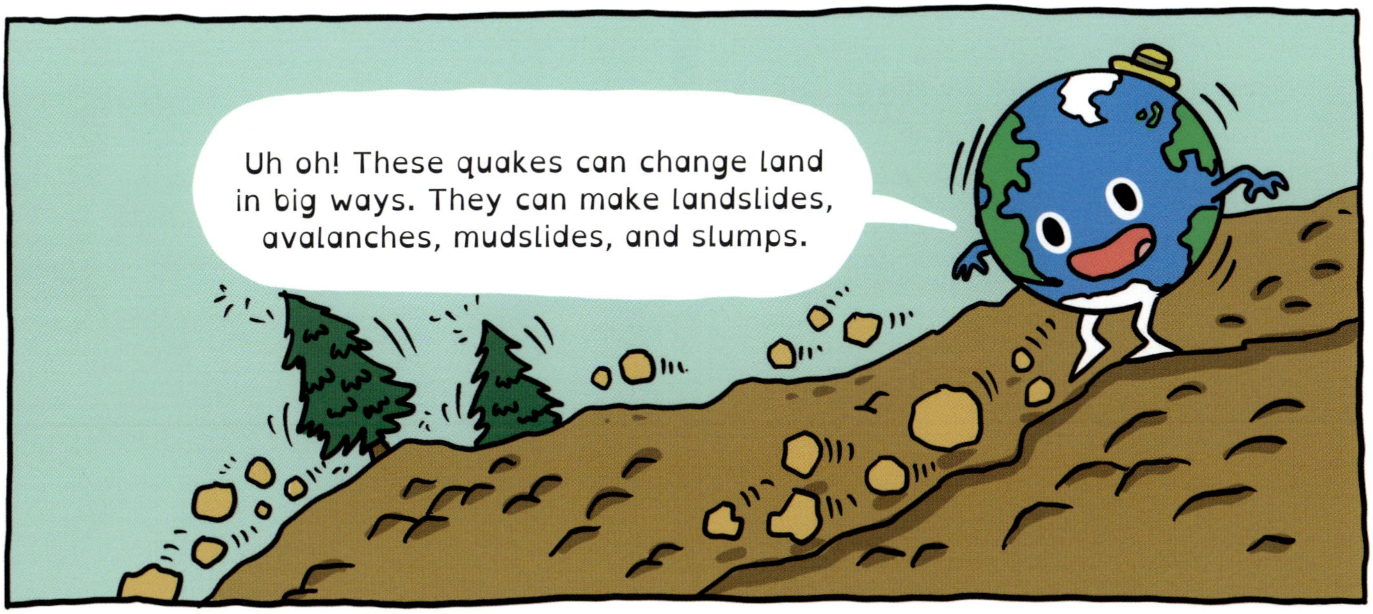
Uh oh! These quakes can change land in big ways. They can make landslides, avalanches, mudslides, and slumps.

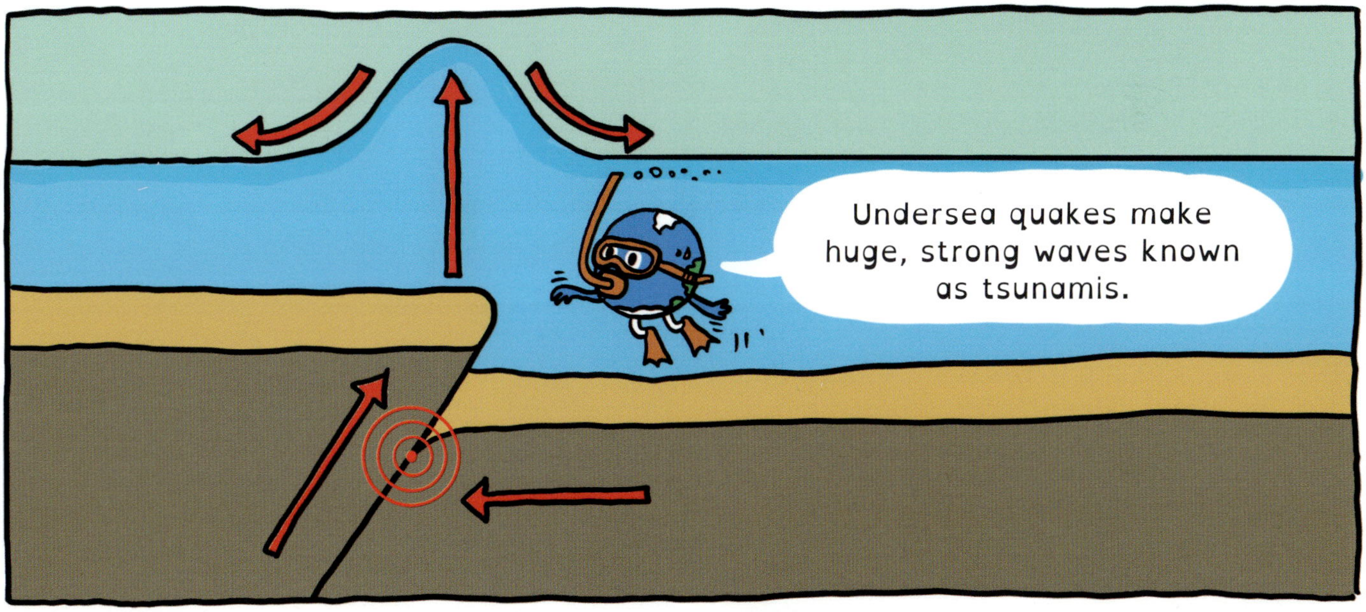
Undersea quakes make huge, strong waves known as tsunamis.

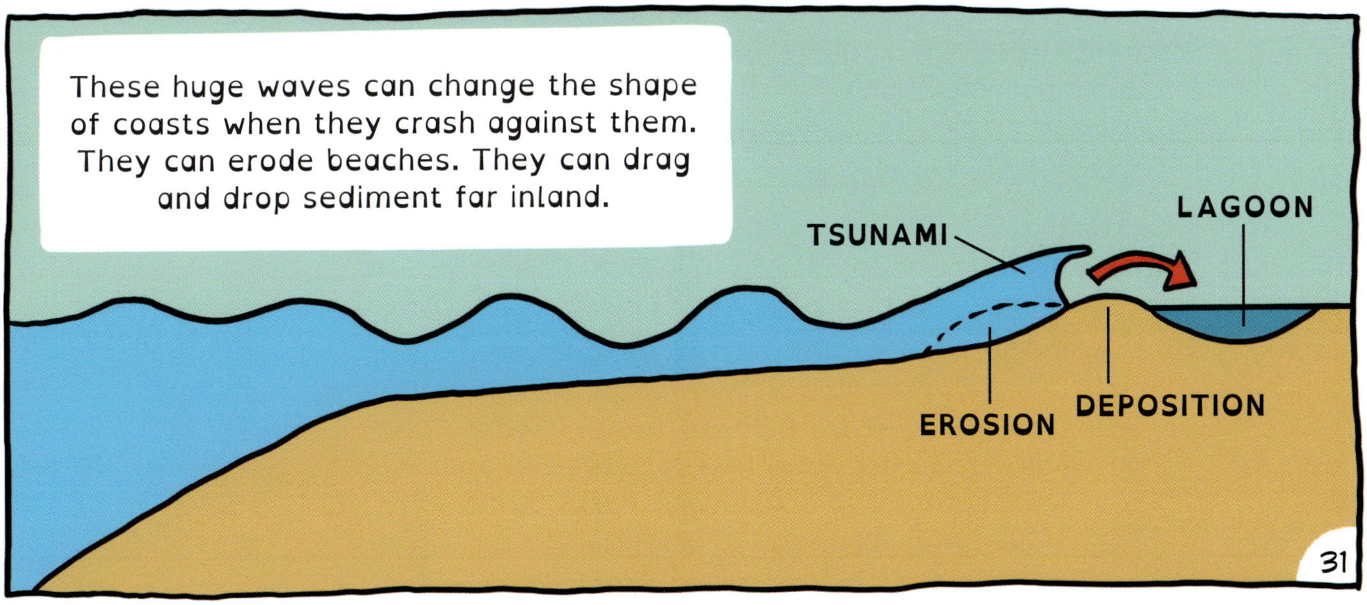
These huge waves can change the shape of coasts when they crash against them. They can erode beaches. They can drag and drop sediment far inland.
TSUNAMI
LAGOON
EROSION
DEPOSITION

HUMAN ACTIVITIES THAT CHANGE EARTH

Hey, watch it, pal! It's not just natural forces that can change land. Humans change it in huge ways, too.
People cut trees, mow plains, drain wetlands, and water deserts to make room for farms. Much of my land is changed due to agriculture.
These days, I don't look much like me.
Tree and plant roots help hold soil in place. When forests get cut for wood, wind and rain can erode that new loose soil.
When people burn **fossil fuels,** it can make acid rain. Rain like this speeds up weathering and erosion on rocks such as limestone, chalk, and marble.
fossil fuels: FAH-suhl FYOOLZ

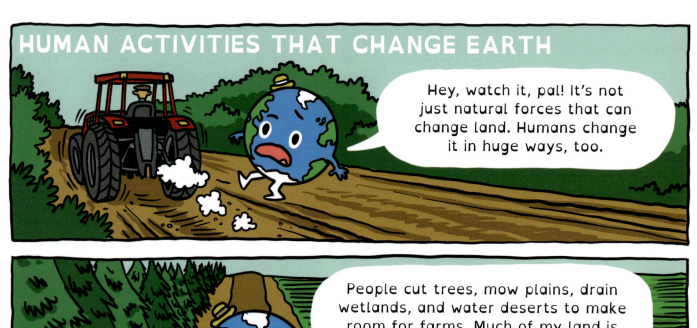

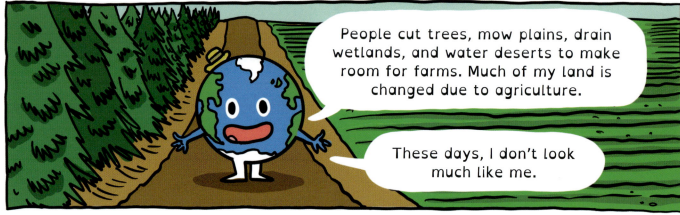

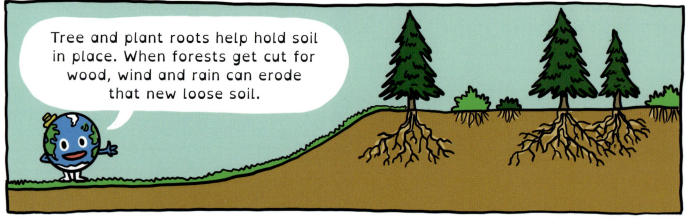

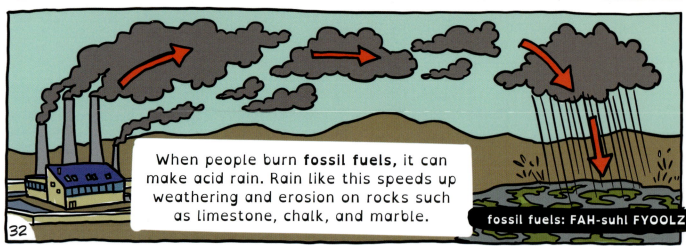

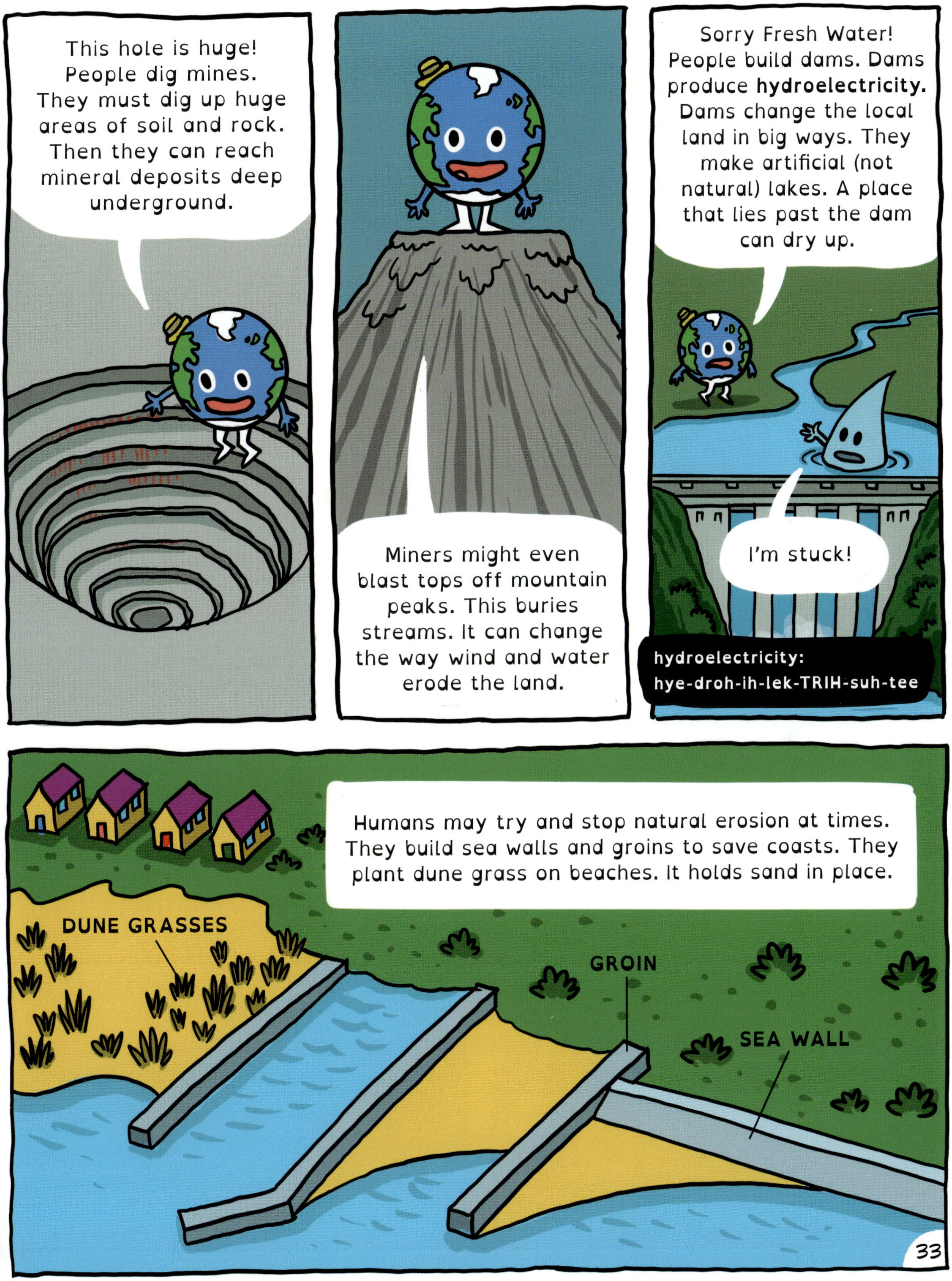
This hole is huge! People dig mines. They must dig up huge areas of soil and rock. Then they can reach mineral deposits deep underground.
Miners might even blast tops off mountain peaks. This buries streams. It can change the way wind and water erode the land.
Sorry Fresh Water! People build dams. Dams produce hydroelectricity. Dams change the local land in big ways. They make artificial (not natural) lakes. A place that lies past the dam can dry up.
I'm stuck!
hydroelectricity: hye-droh-ih-lek-TRIH-suh-tee
Humans may try and stop natural erosion at times. They build sea walls and groins to save coasts. They plant dune grass on beaches. It holds sand in place.
DUNE GRASSES
GROIN
SEA WALL

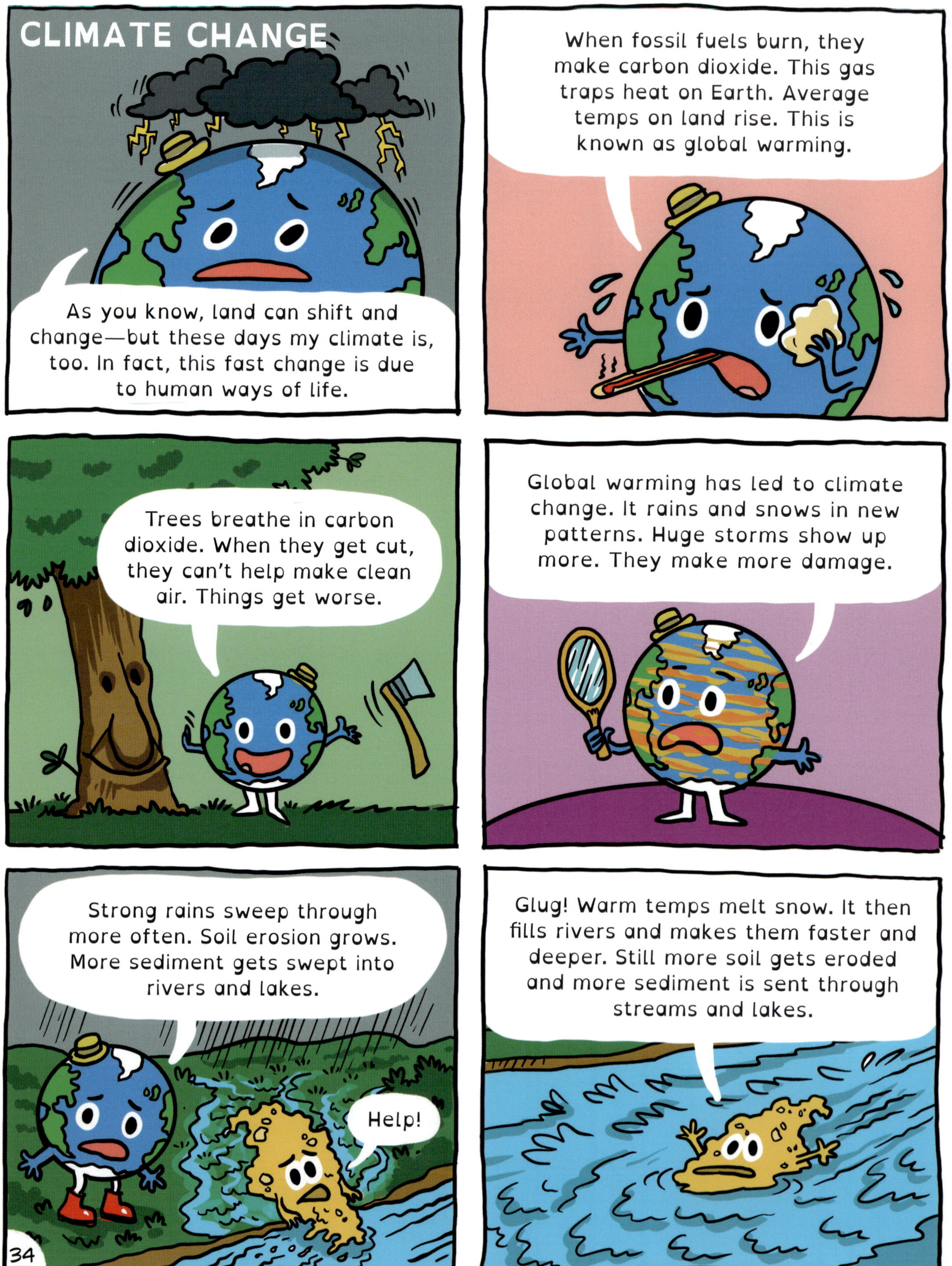
CLIMATE CHANGE
As you know, land can shift and change—but these days my climate is, too. In fact, this fast change is due to human ways of life.
When fossil fuels burn, they make carbon dioxide. This gas traps heat on Earth. Average temps on land rise. This is known as global warming.
Trees breathe in carbon dioxide. When they get cut, they can't help make clean air. Things get worse.
Global warming has led to climate change. It rains and snows in new patterns. Huge storms show up more. They make more damage.
Strong rains sweep through more often. Soil erosion grows. More sediment gets swept into rivers and lakes.
Help!
Glug! Warm temps melt snow. It then fills rivers and makes them faster and deeper. Still more soil gets eroded and more sediment is sent through streams and lakes.

This is not good! Climate change brings strong storms that speed up erosion on coasts.
This bear needs its ice back!
Sea ice that melts in the Arctic Ocean is on the rise. In summer, 10% more melts each decade since 1978.
Seas rise when ice sheets melt. Lots keep melting. They melt at the poles. They melt on mountain peaks. Low islands and low coasts are at risk around the globe
Humans can help. They can make new ways of life. They can leave smaller **"carbon footprints."**
carbon footprints: KAR-buhn FUHT-prints
You can switch which kind of energy you use. You can use sun and wind power. You will not need to burn fossil fuels then. Less carbon dioxide will fill the air.
You can eat less meat, too. Cattle lets off methane gas—lots of it. That gas traps heat, too. When people raise cattle, it may mean that they cut trees and forests. This makes room for animals to graze.

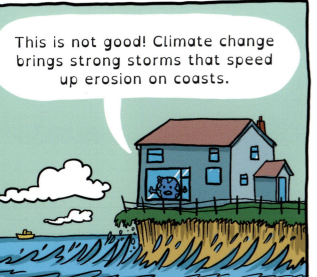

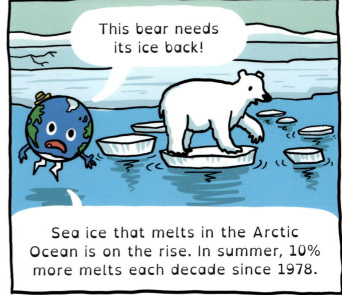

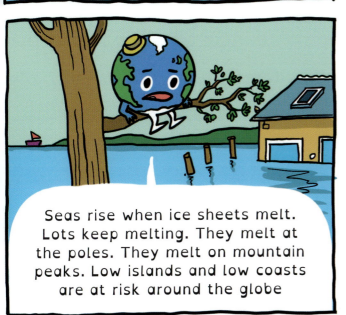

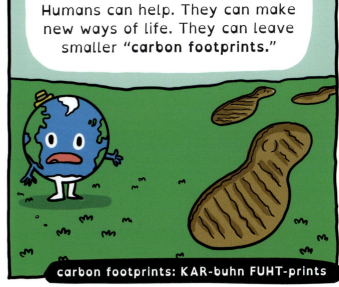

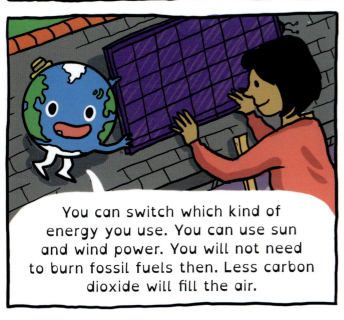

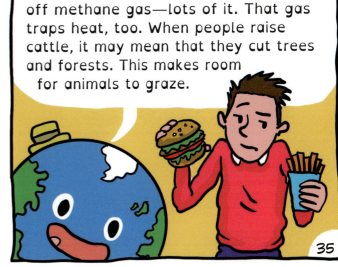

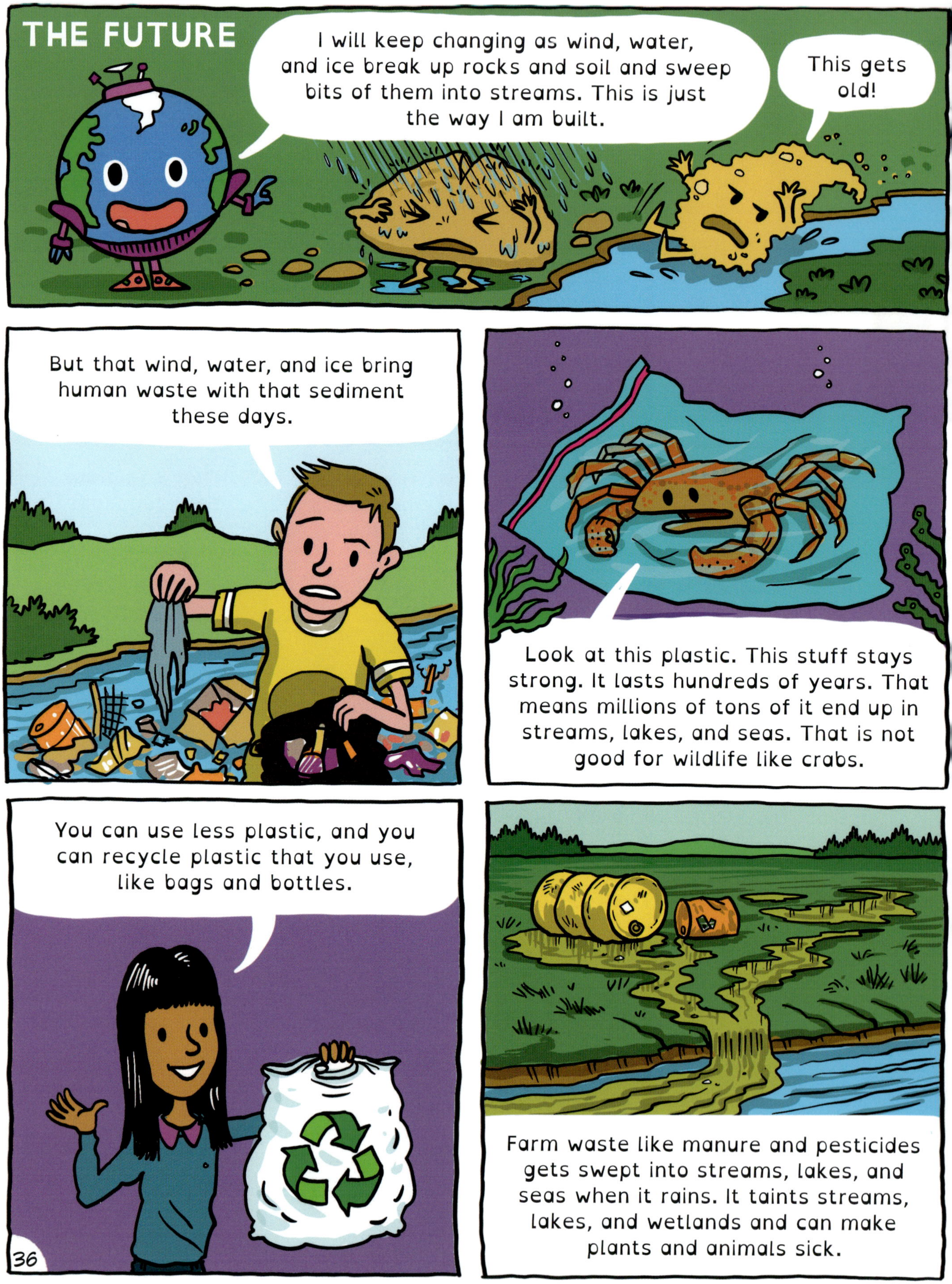
THE FUTURE
I will keep changing as wind, water, and ice break up rocks and soil and sweep bits of them into streams. This is just the way I am built.
This gets old!
But that wind, water, and ice bring human waste with that sediment these days.
Look at this plastic. This stuff stays strong. It lasts hundreds of years. That means millions of tons of it end up in streams, lakes, and seas. That is not good for wildlife like crabs.
You can use less plastic, and you can recycle plastic that you use, like bags and bottles.
Farm waste like manure and pesticides gets swept into streams, lakes, and seas when it rains. It taints streams, lakes, and wetlands and can make plants and animals sick.

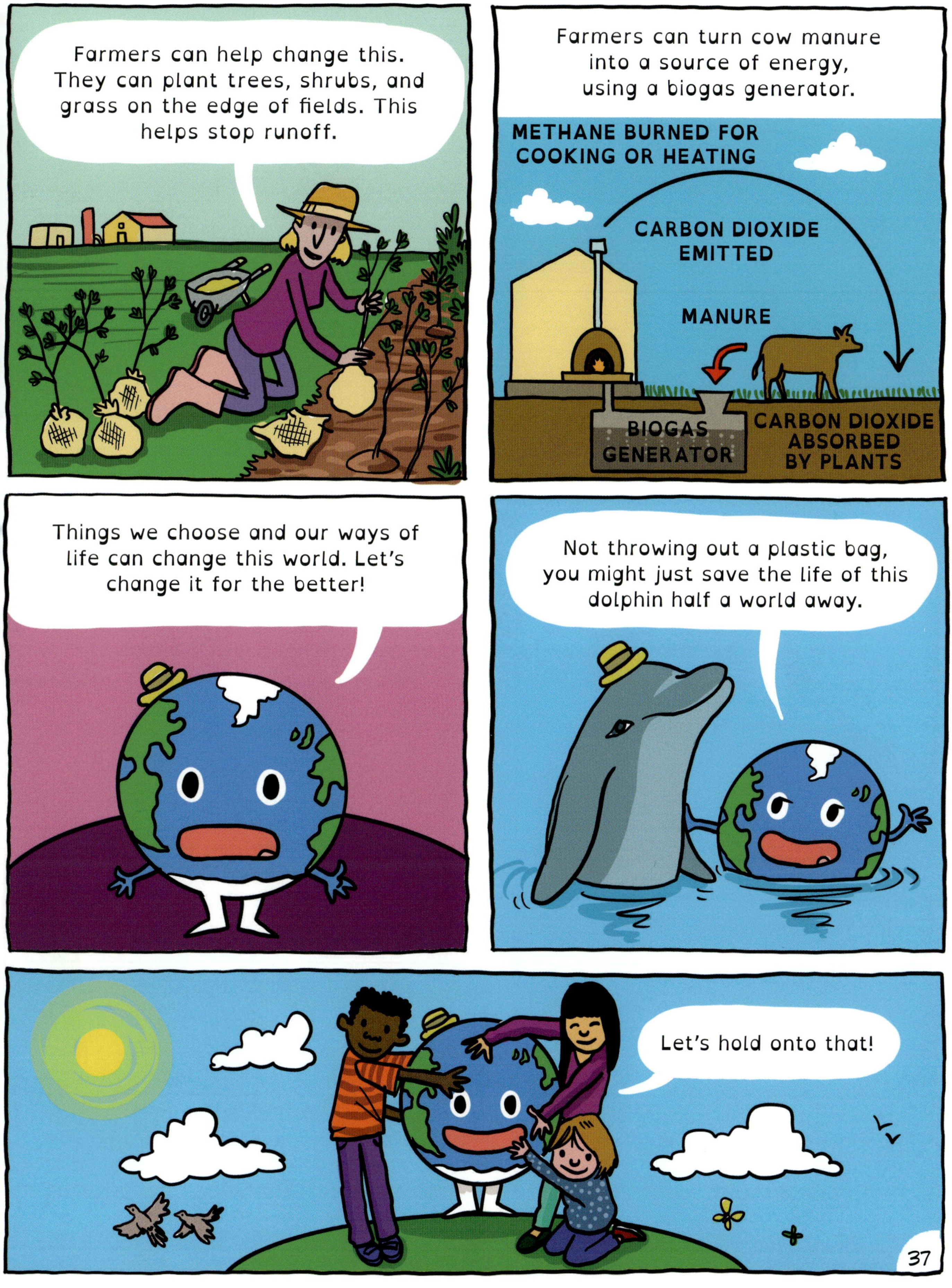

Farmers can help change this. They can plant trees, shrubs, and grass on the edge of fields. This helps stop runoff.
Farmers can turn cow manure into a source of energy, using a biogas generator.
METHANE BURNED FOR COOKING OR HEATING
CARBON DIOXIDE EMITTED
MANURE
BIOGAS GENERATOR
CARBON DIOXIDE ABSORBED BY PLANTS
Things we choose and our ways of life can change this world. Let's change it for the better!
Not throwing out a plastic bag, you might just save the life of this dolphin half a world away.
Let's hold onto that!

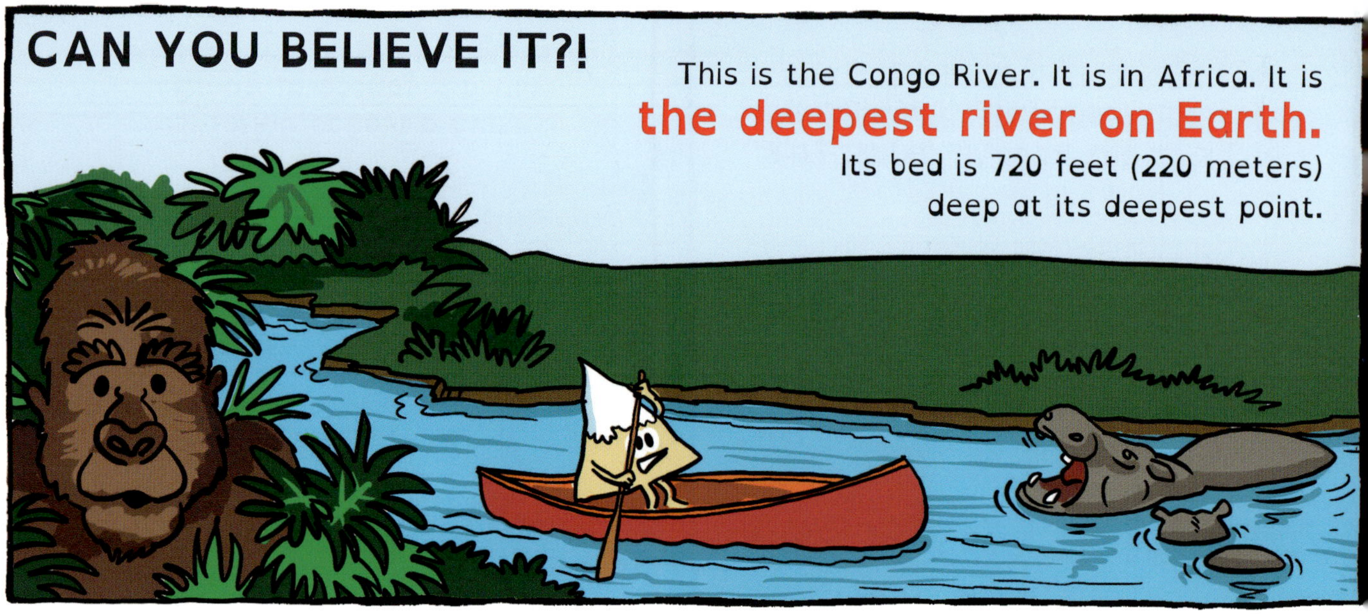
CAN YOU BELIEVE IT?!
This is the Congo River. It is in Africa. It is
the deepest river on Earth.
Its bed is 720 feet (220 meters) deep at its deepest point.

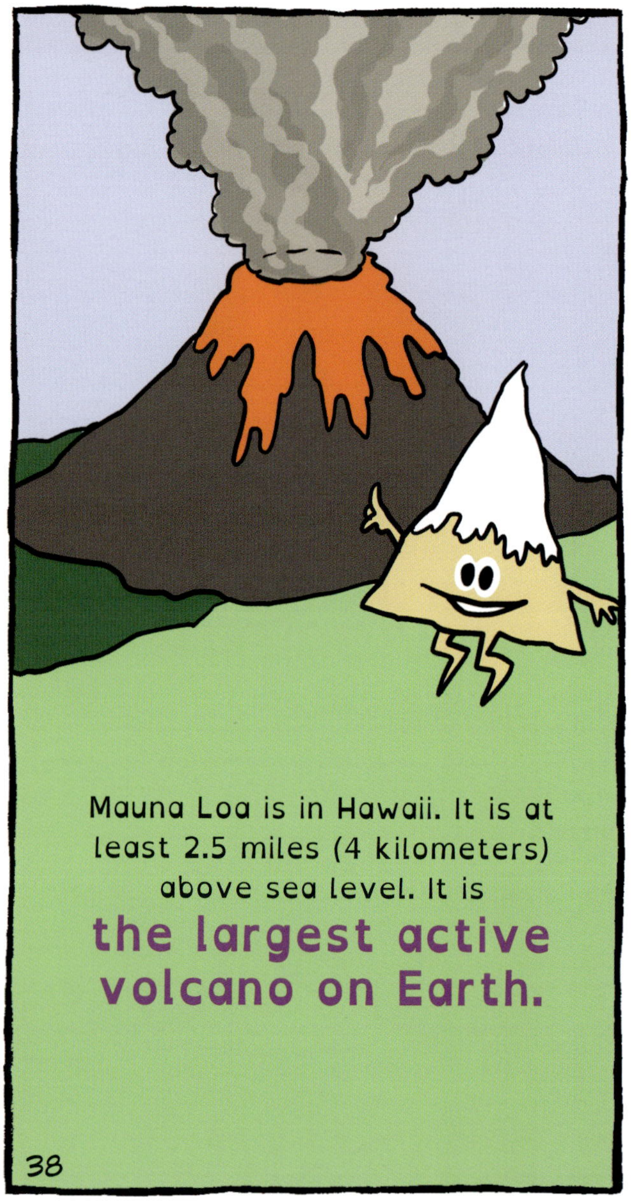
Mauna Loa is in Hawaii. It is at least 2.5 miles (4 kilometers) above sea level. It is
the largest active volcano on Earth.

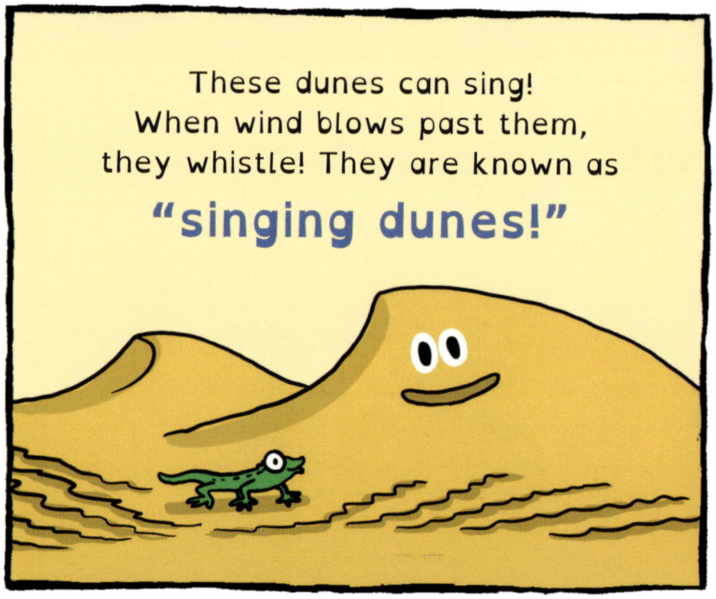
These dunes can sing! When wind blows past them, they whistle! They are known as
"singing dunes!"

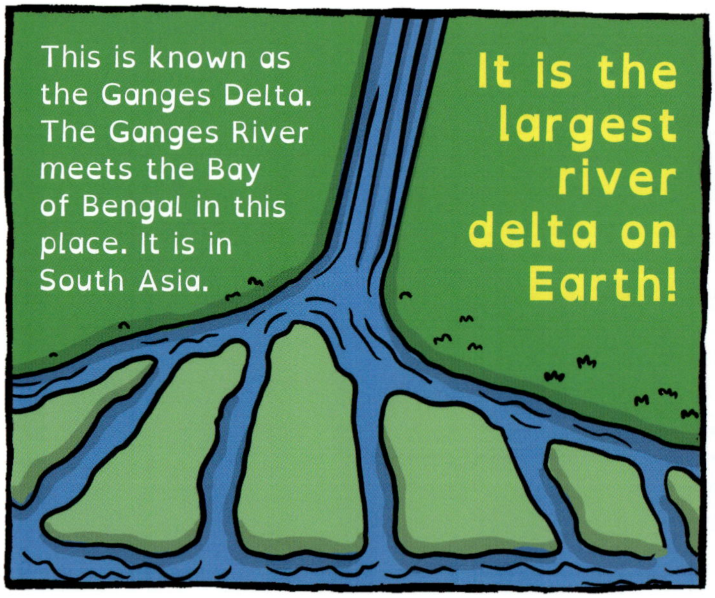
This is known as the Ganges Delta. The Ganges River meets the Bay of Bengal in this place. It is in South Asia.
It is the largest river delta on Earth!

This ice sheet is in Greenland. It is known as **Jakobshavn Isbrae**. It is **the fastest glacier on Earth.** It can reach a top speed of close to 130 feet (40 meters) in a day.

The Denman glacier in Antarctica flows on top of a huge land canyon. It is at least 11,000 feet (3,500 meters) below sea level. That makes it **the deepest land canyon on Earth!**

Indonesia has the **most active volcanoes** of any country on Earth. You can find at least **139 active volcanoes** in this place!

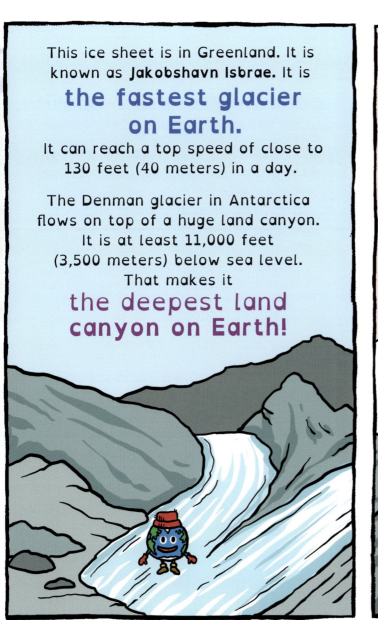

When this quake shook 100 miles (160 kilometers) off Chile's coast, it broke records! That is in South America. It took place on May 22, 1960. It was **the most powerful quake** ever recorded. It made the sea shake and rise. It made a tsunami. That huge wave struck the town of Hilo, Hawaii.

WORDS TO KNOW

bank the rising ground bordering a river or stream.

carbon footprint the amount of carbon dioxide emitted due to the use of fossil fuels by a particular person, group, or activity.

cove a small bay.

crater a bowl-shaped opening, often found at the top of a volcano.

crest the highest points on a ripple, wave, ridge, or dune.

fissure a long, narrow opening or crack.

fossil fuels sources of energy that formed from the remains of living things that died millions of years ago. Coal, oil, and natural gas are fossil fuels.

gradient a slope.

hydroelectricity electric energy generated using the motion of falling or flowing water.

lava molten rock that pours out of volcanoes or from cracks in Earth.

load the total amount of sediment carried by a river or stream.

sedimentary rock rock formed by the accumulation and compression of layers of sediment over time.

tectonic plate a massive, irregular-shaped slab of rock, usually composed of continental and oceanic crust. Earth's surface is made up of about 30 tectonic plates.

trough the lowest point between ridges or dunes.

undulating rising and falling.

water table the level below which the ground is saturated with water.

40